Beyond Self-Care

Leading a Systemic
Approach to Well-Being
for Educators

GAIL MARKIN

Foreword by Sabre Cherkowski

Solution Tree | Press

Copyright © 2023 by Solution Tree Press

Materials appearing here are copyrighted. With one exception, all rights are reserved. Readers may reproduce only those pages marked "Reproducible." Otherwise, no part of this book may be reproduced or transmitted in any form or by any means (electronic, photocopying, recording, or otherwise) without prior written permission of the publisher.

555 North Morton Street
Bloomington, IN 47404
800.733.6786 (toll free) / 812.336.7700
FAX: 812.336.7790

email: info@SolutionTree.com
SolutionTree.com

Visit **go.SolutionTree.com/educatorwellness** to download the free reproducibles in this book.

Printed in the United States of America

Library of Congress Cataloging-in-Publication Data

Names: Markin, Gail, author.
Title: Beyond self-care : leading a systemic approach to well-being for educators / Gail Markin.
Description: Bloomington, IN : Solution Tree Press, [2022] | Includes bibliographical references and index.
Identifiers: LCCN 2022023013 | ISBN 9781954631274 (Paperback) | ISBN 9781954631281 (eBook)
Subjects: LCSH: Teachers--Health and hygiene. | Teaching--Psychological aspects. | Self-care, Health. | Stress management. | Well-being. | Educational leadership--Social aspects.
Classification: LCC LB3415 .M366 2022 | DDC 371.1--dc23/eng/20220930
LC record available at https://lccn.loc.gov/2022023013

Solution Tree
Jeffrey C. Jones, CEO
Edmund M. Ackerman, President

Solution Tree Press
President and Publisher: Douglas M. Rife
Associate Publisher: Sarah Payne-Mills
Managing Production Editor: Kendra Slayton
Editorial Director: Todd Brakke
Art Director: Rian Anderson
Copy Chief: Jessi Finn
Production Editor: Alissa Voss
Content Development Specialist: Amy Rubenstein
Acquisitions Editor: Sarah Jubar
Copy Editor: Evie Madsen
Proofreader: Elisabeth Abrams
Text and Cover Designer: Laura Cox
Associate Editor: Sarah Ludwig
Editorial Assistants: Charlotte Jones and Elijah Oates

To healing and hope . . .

Acknowledgments

I would like to acknowledge that I wrote this book on the traditional and unceded lands of the Matsqui, Kwantlen, Katzie, and Semiahmoo First Nations. I am grateful for their stewardship.

It is difficult to know where to begin as this is a book of collective wisdom. I see my role as putting the research together with stories of people's practice and experiences. I am grateful for the stories and ideas others shared with me, and I take the responsibility of this gift very seriously. I hope I serve you well.

I want to start with thanking my parents, Angus and Jacolyn Currie, and my siblings, AnneLouise, Diane, Iain, and Donna, who taught me what it means to belong, love unconditionally, and always lift up one another.

Thanks to my childhood-and-beyond friends, Candice, Carolynn, Jill, and Linda, who continue to teach me about friendship and challenge my thinking and feeling with great debate and curiosity. Thanks to my parenting buddy, Connie, and all of the 8-96 hockey moms who are my cheering squad and the people I know I could call on for anything, anytime.

A special thanks also to the Williams Lake crew, Ann, Shane, Laurie, and my soul sister MaryAnne. You were my first work team and taught me what a great team should feel like and that relationship matters. I love our friendship and that we will grow old together still dancing.

Speaking of dancing, thanks also to my Project Parent team. Thanks for getting me through those beautiful, busy parenting years. I remember so much amazing work and so much fun, connection, and laughter. You are the best!

A special thank you to all my educational work teams. You are doing such amazing and holy work. I hope you will see and hear your stories in this book and that

I have told them with the love and care they deserve. There are a few particular friends and colleagues who helped me with this book and asked not to be named here; please know I am immensely grateful to you.

Thank you to my friends and brilliant colleagues doing this well-being work with me on the British Columbia (BC) School Centred Mental Health Coalition, Social-Emotional Learning (SEL) BC, Compassionate Systems Leadership Network, and the K–12 Staff Wellbeing BC Network. This book is a compilation of members' wisdom. I can't name you all, but I know you know who you are, and I hope you know how much you mean to me.

Thanks to my academic inspirations and mentors, particularly Fei Wang, Sabre Cherkowski, and Kimberly A. Schonert-Reichl. Thanks also to the amazing students of the 2020 pandemic cohort of the University of British Columbia Doctorate in Educational Leadership and Policy program I have been learning alongside. They are all such great leaders, learners, and teachers.

A huge thank you and love always to my children—or, as my dad would have said, "my adult offspring"—Courtney and Aaron. You are always my inspiration to do things better. Thank you for all your encouragement, love, and support. My final and biggest thank you to my husband, Tony, who has supported me through this work and always encouraged me to keep going. I am so grateful to live this beautiful life with you.

—Gail Markin

Solution Tree Press would like to thank the following reviewers:

Kim Ballestro
Assistant Principal
Carterville Junior High School
Carterville, Illinois

Kendra Bell
Chief Academic Support Officer
Peoria Unified School District
Peoria, Arizona

Sabre Cherkowski
Professor, Director of
　Graduate Programs
University of British Columbia
Kelowna, British Columbia, Canada

Doug Crowley
Assistant Principal
DeForest Area High School
DeForest, Wisconsin

John D. Ewald
Education Consultant
Frederick, Maryland

Doug Gee
Superintendent
Clear Lake Community
　School District
Clear Lake, Iowa

Peter Johnston
Director of Professional Learning and Development
BC Principals' and Vice-Principals' Association
Vancouver, British Columbia, Canada

Jeff Lahey
Assistant Principal
Flower Mound High School
Flower Mound, Texas

Ian Landy
Principal
Powell River School District
Powell River, British Columbia, Canada

Peter Marshall
Elementary School Principal
Halton District School Board
Burlington, Ontario, Canada

Elizabeth Nowlan
Principal
Maplehurst Middle School
Moncton, New Brunswick, Canada

Janet Nuzzie
District Instructional Specialist, K–12 Mathematics Intervention
Pasadena Independent School District
Pasadena, Texas

Tanya Rogers
Principal
Aberdeen Elementary
Kamloops, British Columbia, Canada

Nadine Trépanier-Bisson
Director of Professional Learning
Ontario Principals' Council
Toronto, Ontario, Canada

Kim Weatherby
School Health Promotion Consultant
Victoria, British Columbia, Canada

Visit **go.SolutionTree.com/educatorwellness** to download the free reproducibles in this book.

Table of Contents

Reproducible pages are in italics.

About the Author xi
Foreword xiii
Introduction 1
    Why Educators Are Not All Right 2
    Why I Wrote This Book 3
    About This Book 4

1 The *Why*: Why Well-Being Matters 9
    Social-Emotional Learning and Well-Being 10
    Health, Happiness, and Success at Work 13
    The Business Case for Well-Being 18
    The Bottom Line 20

2 The *Self*: The Beauty of and Problems With Self-Care 23
    The Traditional Approach to Self-Care 23
    The Bandage on the Elephant 25
    Ways to Share Effective Self-Care Practices 26
    Self-Care Begins With Being Self-Aware 30
    The Bottom Line 39
    Steps to Build and Use Self-Awareness 41
    Steps to Build External Self-Awareness 44

3 The *Other*: Social Connection and Belonging 45
    The Need to Belong 47
    Relationship-Based Workplaces 52
    Belonging Cues and Action Strategies 54
    A Culture of Connection, Not Competition 60

Negativity Bias and Inaccurate Stories. 63
　　　The Bottom Line. 64
　　　Check-In Protocol for Building Self-Awareness, Team Connection,
　　　　and Belonging 67
　　　Protocol for Appreciative Inquiry 68
　　　Identifying Negativity Bias and Determining Actions and Belonging Cues 70

4　The *Other*: Psychological Safety. 71
　　　A Psychologically Safe Workplace .72
　　　Psychological Safety, Defined 76
　　　The Fallible Leader. 91
　　　The Bottom Line 92
　　　Delivering Clear Messages. 94

5　The *System*: Change Is Possible 95
　　　Understand How Systems Impact Well-Being 96
　　　Beware the Quick Fix. 98
　　　Be Clear About the Problem 99
　　　Start With the Low-Hanging Fruit 101
　　　Make Actions Visible. 103
　　　Notice and Name Subversive Leadership Practices 104
　　　Break Down Big Problems, Ask Questions, and Give Feedback 107
　　　Embed Structures That Support Well-Being 108
　　　The Bottom Line. 110
　　　Focus Group Questions and Considerations 112

Conclusion. **113**
References and Resources **115**
Index **125**

About the Author

 **Gail Markin** is a counselor and teacher who has worked to support health and well-being in her local school district in Langley, British Columbia (BC), and across the province. Gail began her career as a social worker, family counselor, and parent educator. After becoming a teacher, Gail worked as a school counselor in many schools before moving to her district support role. As an educational consultant promoting staff well-being, Gail is particularly proud of a project she did in conjunction with BC Children's Hospital, where she worked with rural and remote school districts to support health and well-being.

Gail is the chair of Social Emotional Learning (SEL) BC and a member of the steering committee of the BC School Centred Mental Health Coalition. Gail participates in two amazing communities of practice that help shape her work: the K–12 Staff Wellbeing Network and the Compassionate Systems Leadership Network. It is through these supportive and connected networks that Gail developed her passion for spreading her message about the importance of well-being, which she does through writing, teaching, and speaking. Gail has written articles for the BC School Superintendents Association, the BC School Counsellors Association, the BC Principals' and Vice-Principals' Association, and the EdCan Network. Gail also coauthored a book chapter for new school administrators with Fei Wang, associate professor at the Faculty of Education, the University of British Columbia.

Speaking and presenting energize Gail. As a big podcast fan, Gail enjoyed being a podcast guest as well as a co-host of the *Where You Are* podcast (https://whereyouarepodcast.com). Gail is particularly proud of her 2019 TEDx Talk on the power of belonging.

Gail has two bachelor's degrees and two master's degrees in psychology and education. She is working on a doctorate in leadership and policy at the University of British Columbia.

To learn more about Gail's work, visit GailMarkin.ca or follow @MarkinGail on Twitter.

To book Gail Markin for professional development, contact pd@SolutionTree.com.

Foreword

By Dr. Sabre Cherkowski

A saying I have noticed playing out in my life and my work as an educator and researcher is *The teacher will show up when learning is needed.* Gail Markin's book, *Beyond Self-Care: Leading a Systemic Approach to Well-Being for Educators*, shows up as a teacher for the needed learning in our school systems, providing K–12 school leaders with a research-informed approach to building well-being for themselves, others, and the systems within which they work. Educators are at a time of high stress, burnout, and disease as they navigate work and life environments often characterized by volatility, uncertainty, complexity, and ambiguity. As Gail reminds us in the opening chapter, well-being matters not only for the students, who are in the care of teachers, leaders, and all school staff, but also for those adults in the building, who deserve to be well at work. This book offers encouragement for leaders as they tackle the hard and important work of building structures for well-being in their schools and systems.

I first met Gail several years ago through my research on flourishing in schools. She is now as she was then—committed to sharing with others what she is learning about her passion and purpose of growing well-being for all in schools. Throughout this book, Gail calls on readers to notice well-being across the education system, highlighting the interconnectedness of well-being at the levels of self, others, and system. Leaders learn first about the importance of practicing self-care at work from recent research and writing in the fields of positive psychology, business, health, and social-emotional learning (SEL). As I have found in my research on flourishing in schools, as leaders are supported to learn about their own and others' well-being at work, they often shift toward crafting work conditions that nurture and sustain well-being (Cherkowski, Kutsyuruba, & Walker, 2020). Through her book, Gail builds a strong case for the importance of leaders paying attention to well-being at work and offers several sets of tools and strategies that leaders can usefully adapt for different roles, needs, and contexts.

Noting the importance of relationships for effective leadership, she then highlights the centrality of belonging and connection to improve conditions for well-being and powerful teams at work. Gail describes the research on psychological safety and outlines how important it is for leaders to cultivate climates where colleagues feel safe to make mistakes and be open to the learning that can come from these vulnerable moments through giving and receiving feedback. These ideas resonate with my own research findings, in which teachers shared stories of the powerful shift that occurred in their own learning and sense of well-being when their leaders paid attention to building caring relationships, engaging in deep learning with team members, modeling risk-taking, and developing shared norms that created a safer space to share and receive feedback (Cherkowski, Hanson, & Walker, 2018). In this book, Gail offers impactful resources and tools for leaders to build psychological safety through careful and constant attention to growing a sense of belonging and connection for all at work.

In the third part of her model, Gail offers insights and suggestions for system-level perspectives on well-being in schools. Drawing on research and practices in positive psychology and leadership studies and using stories and examples from her long career in education working with administrators and other educators, Gail offers empirical and practical perspectives for moving beyond the self-care focus toward system-level approaches to cultivating well-being in schools. However, Gail reminds us that the learning that is valued in schools for students is not always evident in the school as a workplace. This means that the feedback needed to keep a system growing and improving following inevitable mistakes often fails to make it up the hierarchy of the system if the system does not constantly attend to psychological safety through all parts of itself.

As Gail encourages throughout this book, professional learning for leaders about and for well-being is essential for growing capacity for more well-being in schools (Cherkowski & Walker, 2018; Greenberg, Brown, & Abenavoli, 2016; Mahfouz, 2018). However, establishing well-being as a priority across a school system may be a challenge if leaders have not yet learned or are not supported in their professional learning to build the needed skills and capacities to nurture cultures of well-being, or if they do not believe that this emotional work with their adult colleagues is theirs to do (Crawford, 2009; Montemurro et al., n.d.). Gail notes that research points to the ongoing need to support school leaders in their professional learning toward building, where possible, systemic structures for well-being for themselves and others.

Offering thoughtful ways to practice and implement new knowledge and skills is an important part of the learning process, and this book includes a helpful list of action steps at the end of each chapter. As Gail lays out in the introduction, enacting the recommendations, suggestions, and practices in this book requires courage to inquire deeply into who we are as leaders and how this may be influencing our own well-being and the well-being of others at work. She suggests in the conclusion that we take up the courageous work of leading for well-being from a stance of curiosity and compassion.

Leaders will do well to follow the author's advice of engaging with courage, curiosity, and compassion in an ongoing inquiry of how to build environments of trust, care, and psychological safety that can foster educator well-being. This important inquiry will require support and resources to ensure that well-being remains a primary focus within and across school systems. This book can be one of the supports offered to leaders—a research-informed guide to building the knowledge and practice of well-being in schools as workplaces.

As I write this foreword, it is nearing the end of summer and the start of the school year. This has always felt like an exciting time of year as I look forward to the new opportunities, connections, and possibilities that will come in the new school year. It has also been a time of resting and pausing to reflect on the practices, supports, and resources I will need to sustain the important and difficult work of teaching and leading in education, especially in our increasingly complex, challenging, and uncertain times. For me, books have been a source of knowledge and inspiration for this new year planning. While I may not know the author or the readers of the book, I sometimes feel an invitation to join with them in their commitments and aspirations. This sense of belonging to a group doing important work can embolden and empower me to use what I'm learning in new ways in my work. *Beyond Self-Care* has that sense of invitation into a larger learning community of scholars and practitioners investing in an important, urgent, and worthy commitment—building system-level supports for well-being. I'm excited to join in with this learning community. I hope that, as a reader, you feel the sense of invitation and the urgency to join in the work where you can, in ways that work best for you. As I close out, it seems fitting to end my "New Year" thinking with a toast. So, here's to all of us thinking, acting, and feeling our way forward together, toward well-being for all in our schools.

Introduction

> Well-being is feeling engagement, connection, meaning, positive feelings, and a sense of achievement in life.
> —Martin Seligman

Reflect for a moment on the preceding epigraph quote. As you do, what happens in your body? Do you smile? Do you feel a warmth spread through your body? Do your muscles relax? Maybe, as you are reflecting, you take a slower and deeper breath than you usually would and feel just a little bit more well-being than you did just a moment before. I know this is what happens for me. Now I am smiling and thinking about you smiling, and perhaps you are smiling and thinking about me too. *Well-being* can be as simple as that—a moment of connection between two people over time and space, a release of serotonin in our brains when we smile or share a happy thought.

Well-being can also be bigger and more active, of course. The *runner's high* is a state of well-being, as is the joy of creating a beautiful piece of art or watching your child dance, skate, or walk down the aisle. It can be a moment or a longer experience of joy or engagement, but it is not a permanent state—no one is in a constant state of well-being. Despite this, all people know what it feels like when they are generally well at work and in life—and when they are not.

Over the next few chapters, I will take a deep dive into the challenges with educator well-being, the traditional strategies leaders use to improve well-being, and the research and tools available now to truly help educators thrive both in and out of the workplace. You will discover the well-being triad and learn how the interplay of three factors influences educator well-being. And you will discover tools that can help you, as a leader, improve not only your well-being but also that of the people you work with. So let's dive in!

Why Educators Are Not All Right

Start with the *Sunday night test* to gauge your well-being. How do you feel on Sunday nights when you are thinking about the week ahead? When you look at the calendar for the following week, what goes on for you? Are you excited, sick to your stomach, or somewhere in between? What about the rest of your team? Is there a tally on the staff room bulletin board counting down the days to spring break from the minute you return after winter break? Educators—if they know the impacts of chronic stress on people's health, happiness, and success, and they know stress is contagious (Oberle & Schonert-Reichl, 2016)— should be paying attention to what things like the Sunday night test and other, admittedly more scientific, data tell them about well-being in the education system.

Educators go into this beautiful profession full of passion for teaching and learning. They know the powerful impact educators have on the development and growth of students. It is a truly noble and impactful profession. It is because of this impact and the incredible opportunity educators have to make a difference that they owe it to themselves and the communities they serve to nurture that passion and purpose in themselves and one another and to be well. This may sound simple, but it is actually much more complex. Right now, many educators are *not* well.

Fifty-eight percent of teachers report feeling stressed "all of the time" compared to 36 percent in the overall Canadian workforce (Froese-Germain, 2014), and over 40 percent of school leaders report not coping well with their own stress (Wang & Pollock, 2020). A study of the mental health of school staff during the COVID-19 pandemic in British Columbia shows significantly higher rates of psychological distress compared to a representative sample of Canadian adults (Hutchison et al., 2021). Canadian educators are not alone. In a study by the American Federation of Teachers and Badass Teachers Association (2017), 61 percent of teachers report they "always" or "often" find work stressful. A review of principal well-being in Australia finds the pandemic further compounds pre-pandemic issues related to work-life balance, workload intensification, and burnout (Arnold, Rahimi, & Riley, 2021). This book addresses more about the research on stress and other factors that negatively impact educators as individuals and as a group, because educators need to look at and address these very real issues. More importantly, this book provides K–12 administrators a framework and tools that will help leaders move themselves and their teams out of this system of stress and burnout, toward a systemic structure for fostering well-being.

You will learn how to cultivate more well-being in your life and in the lives of others. You will discover why cultivating well-being is so important to the health, happiness, and success of everyone in your organization and why it is even more important for leaders, particularly education leaders, to truly lead this work. Although I wrote this book with school principals and vice-principals in mind, it will be useful for leaders at all levels of traditional educational hierarchies, from teacher leaders and coaches to superintendents. They are the models and teachers for the people they lead.

Workplace well-being, if leaders consider it at all during leadership training programs, is often seen as a *soft skill* or even something separate from or unnecessary in the workplace. Educators have been taught to think of their work lives as different from their "real" lives. However, educators spend the majority of their waking hours in their workplaces. Work is often a place where educators do noble, creative, and important things, where they develop relationships and discover and cultivate their passions and purposes. It can be a place of thriving and flourishing. If things are not going well at work, however, it can also be a place of great pain and soul-wrenching heartbreak.

Why I Wrote This Book

One of the things I love about learning and developing workplace well-being is the interplay of science and soul. I have been interested in psychology and the study of human behavior for years. With two bachelor's degrees, two master's degrees, and a doctorate in progress, I have done a lot of academic learning, which I am incredibly grateful for, but most of my learning and my continued fascination come from my work with people. I have had the opportunity to work in a lot of different workplaces, and so many people and relationships have shaped me. I have worked as a social worker, counselor, teacher, district support teacher, and as an educational consultant for health and well-being with many school districts. I enjoy my work, and, like most educators, I am passionate about the work I do.

Other than one particular time in my life, I could pass the Sunday night test almost every week. Then I started noticing that looking forward to the week ahead was more the exception than the rule. I noticed more of my friends and colleagues struggling to come to work. They were having trouble sleeping, working all hours of the day and night, and living for breaks and weekends. Many were starting to lose the passion that had brought them to education in the first place. My reading of the work of great authors and researchers like Brené Brown (2018), Daniel Coyle (2018), Amy C. Edmondson (2019), Shawn Achor (2018), and others showed me both the negative impacts of stress on people's health and success, and the relatively simple practices that increase well-being. At the same time, I was watching some of the most passionate educators struggling just to make it through the day or even leaving the profession altogether. I wrote this book to share some of this research and put this research together with stories and examples from the field so you have a guidebook to creating and supporting well-being in your schools and workplaces.

Sometimes people ask me why, when I am not a principal, I direct my message to them. It is an excellent question that requires a thoughtful answer. I could start with the fact that I have read the research that tells me principals have a strong influence on the well-being of those they lead (Atasoy, 2020; Çiftgül & Çetinkanat, 2021), and that principals are struggling themselves with increased stress and decreased well-being (Pollock, 2014, 2017; Wang, Pollock, & Hauseman, 2018). After working for and with school administrators since 2007, the more important reason is that as a leader in a few provincial mental health networks, I know both school and district leaders are intensely aware of their responsibility of care and often sacrifice their own well-being to support and care for their teams. As you read this book, you'll discover educators need to support one another to do this work. I hope by sharing the research and compiling the stories, I can add one small piece to this important, collective work on well-being and just maybe take one little thing off your most certainly overloaded plate.

About This Book

This book highlights three components of human behavior: (1) thinking, (2) feeling, and (3) acting (or behavior). If you only stick to the *thinking* part of this book, you will not be disappointed; the science and the business cases for well-being in the workplace really are compelling. You can definitely think your way through this book, but I invite you to dig into the feeling and acting parts as well.

I challenge you to *feel* your way through this book too. Parts of the book will ask you to connect with the material and practices beyond just reading the words on the page. That may involve stopping for a moment and feeling the words you are reading in your body (like you did with the epigraph at the beginning of this introduction), or there may be invitations to remember or visualize something. If you are an education leader, you know connecting at different levels and in different ways to material helps you learn (Rao, 2018), so I invite you to try it.

This book will also be a call to *act*. What actions move leaders and their workplaces toward well-being? What do leaders actually need to do? I invite you to really dig in as you think, feel, and act your way through this book, making it a tool you can read, use, and refer to as you move yourself and your teams toward well-being.

That brings me to the three interconnected parts of well-being: (1) self, (2) other, and (3) system (see figure I.1). These three components create well-being in workplaces (see Compassionate Systems Leadership, n.d.b; K–12 Staff Wellbeing BC Network, n.d.).

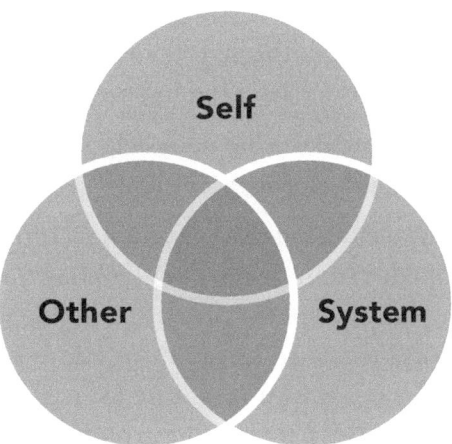

Figure I.1: The three interconnected parts of well-being.

People often think about self-care when others talk about workplace well-being. Looking after yourself and your health is essential for well-being, so I will start there, with the *self*—the first interconnected part of well-being—and address what is helpful about traditional self-care models and where educators need to do better. I will also expand on the traditional model of self-care to include social-emotional learning (SEL) practices like self-awareness and emotional regulation that many organizations teach students, but are often not habits educators intentionally practice as adults. *SELf-care tools* are practices like noticing where you hold feelings in your body or talking to yourself like you would to a good friend when you make a mistake. These tools are simple but hugely impactful practices leaders can use for themselves and model for their teams.

The second part of the triad—*other*—is all about the connection and care people have for one another at work. I will explore the power of belonging and connection and how to harness this power in your work teams. The need for connection is true for *all* successful teams, whether you are leading the district finance department or a school principal leading your school team. The research in this area is fascinating and can help leaders understand which elements contribute to team performance and how to develop, encourage, and model these practices in schools and other workplaces.

The final interconnected and essential part of well-being is the *system*. This is sometimes the part leaders don't get to because it seems too big, or they feel too powerless to make change at a schoolwide or districtwide level. What parts of the system add to your well-being? What parts get in the way? These things may be at any level of your system, from the classroom to the ministry of education or district office. What would happen if you started making your decisions and creating your practices and policies through the lens of well-being? At the systems level, even small changes can have a big impact.

Let's look at how I've structured this book to help support you to think, feel, and act for yourself, others, and your organization.

Chapter 1 discusses why well-being matters and how it directly links to some of the main purposes of education. It reviews the powerful research showing how growing well-being links to success, health, and happiness, and how the well-being of the adults in the system has a direct link to positive student outcomes. This chapter also makes the business case for well-being and shows the direct impact that addressing well-being can have on school and district budgets and staffing challenges.

Chapters 2 through 5 focus on each of the three parts of well-being. Chapter 2 introduces the *self* as the first of the three interconnected parts of well-being. It's about how you can take care of yourself as an individual and how to promote and support self-care as a school or district leader. It explores promising self-care practices and what the research says about these practices and the best ways for leaders to support them. I expand on the traditional physical health concept of self-care many workplaces and human resources departments practice to also include the important social-emotional skills educators know are also important parts of health and well-being.

Chapter 3 introduces the *other* as the second part of well-being; it is about how educators support and lift up one another toward greater success. It's also about the need for connection with others and the importance of belonging. This chapter provides leaders with ways to harness the power of this innate neurobiological need to support and create teams where people are at their best. I will explore what the research says about how belonging and connection can improve well-being and impact group function and performance.

Chapter 4 continues the discussion of *other* with a description of psychological safety and why it is so important to the well-being of individuals and teams. The chapter explains the importance of psychological safety and how leaders can create it, restore it, or both.

Chapter 5 introduces the final part—*system*—and is about how leaders can make and support systemic change. Through research and examples, this chapter describes ways to have impacts on the system that are immediately actionable and which may appear like small changes, but actually have significant impact. This chapter also describes working toward larger systems change and how to move that work forward and make the changes sustainable over time.

A conclusion shares a call for educators to work intentionally together, and provides a summary of the importance of having all three parts working together.

All three interconnected parts of this work (self, other, and system) will take courage—courage to reflect on your own practice, explore and ask questions, and try new things. This book invites you to feel, think, and take action toward well-being in your workplace. Are you ready to dive in with me?

The *Why*
Why Well-Being Matters

> We should not need to rely on our families to support us to get through the day at work. Instead, our workplace should be so supportive that when we go home, we have the energy we need to care for them.
> —Pippa Rowcliffe (personal communication, February 20, 2020)

Why does workplace well-being matter? There are so many important answers to that question, starting with the main purpose of the work: *students' education*. Since 1994, when I started leading social-emotional learning (SEL) workshops, I have asked groups of parents and teachers questions like, "What do you want for your children?" and "When they leave your home or your school system and head out into the adult world, what are your hopes for them?" The answers are always similar—things like successful and loving relationships, good health, successful and fulfilling careers, or contributing to the world in a positive way. Everyone wants students and children to grow up to be happy, healthy, and successful adults who contribute to the world in their own unique way.

As students and children join the workforce, people want workplaces to be healthy spaces for two reasons: (1) to model healthy workplaces for the next generation and (2) to create places where adults can also grow and thrive because the adults in the building matter too. Leaders in education want everyone in the organizations to thrive, and for good reason. Perhaps the most compelling reason author and inspirational speaker Simon Sinek (2014) beautifully sums up is, "Returning from work feeling inspired, safe, fulfilled, and grateful is a natural human right to which we are all entitled and not a modern luxury that only a few lucky ones are able to find" (p. 16).

French philosopher Paul Ricœur (1992) suggests people deserve to be "aiming at the good life, with and for others in just institutions" (p. 172). Most people understand life cannot always be perfect, but a life where you aim for health, happiness, and success for all seems like a great plan. If this is the hope for students and children, it should not be put aside the moment students and children become adults and join the workforce.

In this chapter, I begin by looking at the SEL skills that affect well-being, including well-being in daily life. I then take a deep dive into the neuroscience behind health, happiness, and success at work, and ultimately make the business case for why well-being at work is worth a leader's time, effort, and investment.

Social-Emotional Learning and Well-Being

Positive psychology and SEL research show there are specific social and emotional skills educators can teach that are predictive of increased positive outcomes—better health, healthier relationships, and more career and life success.

For example, the Collaborative for Academic, Social, and Emotional Learning (CASEL; 2020) provides the generally accepted definition and description of these skills. Many readers will be familiar with CASEL's (2020) widely used framework, the "CASEL Wheel" (see https://casel.org/casel-sel-framework-11-2020). The core five SEL skills are as follows.

1. **Self-awareness:** The ability to understand one's own emotions, thoughts, and values and how they connect with and influence behavior
2. **Self-management:** The ability to manage or regulate one's own thoughts, feelings, and actions
3. **Social awareness:** The ability to see the perspectives of and to empathize with others
4. **Relationship skills:** The ability to establish and maintain healthy relationships
5. **Responsible decision making:** The ability to make caring and constructive choices for yourself and in social situations

An often-cited meta-analysis of eighty-two research studies involving over 100,000 students shows that teaching these SEL skills can have positive impacts on academics, conduct problems, emotional distress, and drug use up to eighteen years later (Durlak, Weissberg, Dymnicki, Taylor, & Schellinger, 2011). Students who had been taught SEL skills demonstrated an 11-percentile-point gain in academic achievement (Durlak et al., 2011). An update on this and three other meta-analyses on the impact of teaching SEL skills finds similar positive results (Mahoney, Durlak, & Weissberg, 2018). This alone should be enough for educators, parents, and anyone involved in education to realize the value of teaching and learning these skills.

Many schools now teach these SEL skills to students (Cohen, Opatosky, Savage, Stevens, & Darrah, 2021), but this is a relatively new practice in education, and *many adults themselves were never taught these skills*. For example, when I ask adults what messages they received about feelings in their own families, they often tell stories about keeping a stiff upper lip, not talking about feelings, or some feelings being OK and others not. Many educators learned these SEL *soft skills* were signs of weakness, and that feelings do not belong in the workplace. My own dad, who was the sweetest, gentlest man and fiercely proud of his children, used to brag that no one at work would even know he had children. Family was for warmth, love, and connection, and work was all business and separate from "real" life.

In fact, people spend about 30 percent of their lifetime working, which is a reminder that work life is a significant and important part of people's lives (Statistics Canada, 2019). This statistic is based on a forty-hour work week, so if you are working more than that (like BC principals and vice-principals, for example, who work an average of 56.9 hours a week), you are spending even more of your life at work (Wang & Pollock, 2020).

Putting aside for the moment whether working that much is a good idea, work is a significant part of life. Not only does work account for a lot of your time, well-being, or lack of it, it also does not stay neatly in the workplace. How things go at work and people's wellness there also impact lives outside work. To illustrate, look at the following two examples.

> **Example one:** Vincent, a high school principal, arrives home to his family on a Wednesday evening, yet again at a time later than he hoped. He missed dinner with his family and once again must explain to his wife why he has put his family second to his job. As he is walking upstairs, he steps on a toy car and trips over the dog leash left on the floor. He snaps at his kids. After three days of stress at his school, he has hardly seen his kids, and now his response to a simple toy on the floor is to yell at his children. The ache in his neck has led to a debilitating headache. He missed lunch again as he was dealing with incident after incident and meeting after meeting at work.
>
> Vincent briefly kisses his wife and explains that he needs to keep working. He grabs the cold food left for him on the table and heads into the den to

catch up on the many emails, messages, and deadlines he has missed over the past few days. He reaches out to some principal colleagues and goes on a negative rant about his school and his district and all the things that are wrong with the system and the people involved. Many hours later, he hits the pillow after an unhealthy snack and a mix of Advil and Tylenol to help with the headache. He lies awake reflecting on how he has entered survival mode—he has literally and figuratively closed his door to students and staff at work and to his family at home. He lies there filled with guilt about the way he responded to a staff member asking for support; he reflects with regret on how he treated his children and left his wife to be a single parent again this week. He sees how his stress is contagious and spreading through his school and his home. How much longer can he do this?

Example two: *Anthony, another high school principal, also arrives home to his family on a Wednesday afternoon. The sun is still out, so he decides to spend some time playing with his kids in the backyard before he helps with dinner. He arrives home happy, with healthy energy to laugh and play with his family. After play and the family dinner, he has time to read with his kids, help with bedtime, spend some time with his wife, and take a few minutes to read or catch up on his favorite TV show. As his head hits the pillow, he reflects on the challenging, yet positive day and is grateful for the engagements he had with students, staff, and his family. He will get a good night's sleep, wake up, and get ready for the day. He will have the patience and energy to engage with staff, senior administrators, and families to plan positive initiatives for the school.*

These two stories are vastly different, yet both are very real; many principals have days and weeks that fall somewhere in the middle of these two scenarios. The important thing to understand is there is no Vincent and no Anthony. Both of these stories are about the same person, the same elementary school principal, the same father—just with different pseudonyms (personal communication, August 8, 2021). These stories are from separate times in this educator's career, in different schools with different cultures. These stories show the impact well-being has on families, and how what happens at work affects people beyond the workday.

I suspect educators can all relate to both Anthony and Vincent, and many of their days are somewhere on that spectrum, so you probably don't need much convincing that how your workday goes impacts the rest of your life and the people around you. But what about your own health, happiness, and success at work? If you know your well-being impacts others, how does the workplace impact you while you are at work?

HEALTH, HAPPINESS, AND SUCCESS AT WORK

How do you feel when you are well at work? Think about one of those times when you were inspired and engaged at work. Take a moment to put yourself back in that situation and think about where you feel that good feeling in your body. What does it feel like? Conversely, what does it feel like when you have had a hard or stressful day at work? Where do you feel that in your body?

> "I hold stress in my neck and shoulder, but the really big stress hits me in the gut. When I heard that my assistant superintendent was coming to visit, I could feel the tension in my body. Everyone knows that unexpected visits aren't positive. When he said that my questions and comments the other day were not OK and that people didn't like working with me, that hit me right in the gut. I just have to think about it to feel that way again, so I try not to think about it."
>
> —Elementary principal (personal communication, August 22, 2021)
>
> "I feel a tightness in my neck and shoulders before every big assembly. I also feel warm, and I know my face is probably all red. It is a combination of worrying about all the things that could go wrong and the excitement of the moment! I know people can tell I am nervous, but my team is there to support me. It is usually better when I notice and can remind myself that we are doing this together and it is going to be fine."
>
> —Elementary principal (personal communication, August 9, 2021)

When I feel stress, it almost always starts in the chest. It feels tight and heavy and has become a huge sign for me that something is going on. All feelings—the good ones and the difficult ones—start in the body. The encouraging news is that human bodies are meant to experience these ups and downs in emotion (Harris, 2019). People have two connected nervous system responses—the *stress response cycle* and the *contagion effect*—that happen naturally when people react to the world around them and are important to understand. The following sections examine these responses.

The Stress Response Cycle

The *sympathetic nervous system* is people's system of arousal that gets them moving and is sometimes referred to as their *stress response* (Russell & Lightman, 2019). The stress response releases the stress hormones *adrenaline* and *cortisol*, which fire up the body system to respond to the environment. This system increases your heart rate, elevates your blood pressure, and boosts the *glucose* (energy supply) in your bloodstream so you are ready to react. *Cortisol* also slows functioning in other areas to preserve energy for the fight-or-flight response by lowering immune system response and suppressing the digestive, reproductive, and growth systems in your body (Russell & Lightman, 2019).

Too much cortisol in your body lowers your immune response, makes you more susceptible to illness, and even lowers your life expectancy (Adam et al., 2017). Read that previous sentence over again. Stress actually *lowers* the number of years you get to live on this planet! Staying in the stress response phase of the cycle without coming back down to normal leads to burnout and illness (Verkuil, Brosschot, Tollenaar, Lane, & Thayer, 2016). Although the surge of cortisol is helpful and a necessary response to keep you safe, your body is not designed to be in this state of arousal all the time; you need to complete the cycle for repair and resilience to occur. If you learn what helps you move your body back to a regular state of arousal, that allows you to stay healthy. Most of the time, this happens naturally; but sometimes, especially if you are not paying attention or are continuously in that state of arousal, you can get stuck there.

Many leaders spend a great deal of time caring for the people around them and don't want to focus on themselves, but if they ignore their body signals, don't take the time to repair, or both, they can end up in a situation like the one Irena, a high school principal, found herself in.

> Blakeview High School was a school in constant chaos, and the school principal, Irena, worked hard to support everyone who struggled, professionally and personally. The stories of what some student families were going through were heartbreaking. She could also see staff struggling with the stress of moving from crisis to crisis, but she felt powerless to stop it. She prided herself on being a positive, strengths-based leader, so she kept trying to look at things through that lens. She tried to convince herself that if she just kept going, things would eventually get better. However, she was ignoring the signs indicating she and many of her staff were burning out. The work was exhausting, and she didn't know what else to do to help. Irena knew she wasn't sleeping well or taking care of her health, but she thought she didn't have time to think about herself.

> When she looks back at it now, she can see she was in the stress response cycle constantly but didn't complete the cycle. Her nervous system was stuck in crisis mode! Irena never did make the decision to take care of herself, but her body decided for her. At the end of a particularly tough day, her administrative assistant found Irena on the floor of her office, and they had to take her out in an ambulance.
>
> Since then, Irena has made changes to ensure she empowers her parasympathetic nervous system to bring her back down from high-stress moments. She is doing much better now that she has learned to listen to her body cues. She regularly reminds herself that she is no good to anyone else if she doesn't take care of herself first.

The good news is that lower levels of this stress response are actually productive (Crum, Salovey, & Achor, 2013). Think about that surge of adrenaline that courses through you when you are inspired and the energy boost that accompanies it. This flood of hormones gets you moving and gives you energy to accomplish tasks. However, this response doesn't last forever. Your *parasympathetic nervous system* works alongside your *sympathetic nervous system* (stress response) to move you in the other direction on the response cycle (Sandvik et al., 2020). It slows you down and helps you return to a more calm and relaxed state that brings your other body systems back to normal levels. The interplay of your sympathetic and parasympathetic nervous systems occurs naturally as you go through your day.

Completing the stress response cycle means allowing the parasympathetic nervous system to kick in and do its job, bringing you back to a regular state of arousal. Often these processes happen instinctually, without a lot of intention, as your body reacts to protect you from real or perceived threats. When the threat is removed, or you realize there is nothing to fear, your body naturally moves through these responses. It is only when you get stuck in this arousal state for long periods that there is a problem. As coauthors and twin sisters Emily Nagoski and Amelia Nagoski (2018) write about burnout, "Stress is not bad for you, being stuck is bad for you" (p. 27).

With practice and intention, you can reduce the amount of time you stay in the heightened state of arousal. When you get stuck or spend too much time in this heightened state, you can also consciously use strategies to bring yourself back down. In chapter 2 (page 23), you will learn more about practical self-care practices you can use to prevent getting stuck or spending too much time in that stress arousal state. These are simple things you already know and do, like moving your body, using full deep breaths to calm your nervous system, and focusing on social connection (Nagoski & Nagoski, 2018). However, you first have to notice it is happening.

There are many books that include excellent self-care practices. Two of my favorites are specifically for educators that friends of mine authored: elementary school educator Morgane Michael's (2022) *From Burnt Out to Fired Up* and instructor, counselor, and facilitator Lisa Baylis's (2021) *Self-Compassion for Educators*. Both are excellent books that describe helpful self-care practices and the research behind them; both books can help you find which activities work best for you. But it still all starts with the need for you to *notice* if or when you are in an elevated arousal state too long or too often and then make a *conscious effort* to come back to equilibrium, allowing your body to rest and repair.

Remember, the goal is not to be in a state of calm all day. People need different levels of energy for different tasks and situations. They want their adrenaline to kick in when they need it (the sympathetic nervous system) and the ability to move through the response cycle afterward (the parasympathetic nervous system). Sometimes your stress response cycle will just kick in as an instinct to protect you, but you can also learn how to react less often to situations where you are safe and move through the cycle more quickly when you do need to. The following is an example of how one middle school principal used intention and awareness of his response cycle to support his work and keep himself well at the same time.

> *Jonas knows his job as a middle school principal is constant and unpredictable; he never knows what the day is going to hold despite what his calendar says. Since he started noticing his body's reactions and how he moves through the stress response cycle, he feels more in control and carries less work stress home with him. To accomplish this, he started taking time during his drive to work to check in with what's going on in his body and arrive in a calm, ready-to-go state. Sometimes he manages to maintain that feeling for a while, but it often doesn't last long as his day gets going. Sometimes he is the opposite of calm, but in his job, he needs that adrenaline boost too.*
>
> *When Jonas hears a student screaming and swearing down the hall, his adrenaline kicks in. It happens automatically; he doesn't have to think about it at all. When he averts that crisis, he tries to take a moment to notice the situation has changed (calmed) and lets his nervous system return to a calmer state. Even just taking a moment to notice his body's response and take a breath or two is enough. Or sometimes, when he notices an increased heart rate and tense muscles, he can redirect that adrenaline to another task. Then he is ready for whatever else may come his way. The days he is not intentional or fails to note his body's response, he can stay elevated all day—and that is not good for anyone.*

Like Jonas, as educators grow and develop, they become more proficient and are able to move through the two connected systems more easily, and more brain connections form. It is like exercise for the body—the more you exercise this response cycle, the easier it is for you to manage it, move more easily through different states of arousal, and recover from difficult events in your life. This type of exercise is the building block of resilience.

The Contagion Effect

Understanding the stress response cycle and practicing ways to move through it are important to avoid burnout and keep yourself healthy. The other important thing to know about stress: it's contagious. A classroom study where researchers compared the self-reported stress levels of teachers with saliva samples containing cortisol (a stress hormone) from their students finds as the teachers' level of stress went up, so too did the levels of cortisol in the students (Oberle & Schonert-Reichl, 2016). This study is correlational; it doesn't tell which came first—the teacher's stress or the students' cortisol—but in many ways, it doesn't really matter. It does say stress is contagious and that your stress level has an impact on both yourself and others. This is also true in the workplace, where research shows moods are contagious and moods of group members—particularly leaders—affect group behaviors and outcomes (Sy & Choi, 2013).

The problem for your health comes not when you have a stress response but when you stay in that response too long.

This *contagion effect* means when you are well, it also positively impacts the health, happiness, and success of the people around you. People are social beings, and their happiness is like a snowball increasing in size as it rolls downhill—it just keeps incrementally building up the benefits. When you are healthy and feel happy and inspired, you come to work and work productively and get along with others. For leaders, the impact of this contagion effect is even more powerful, and when you are doing well, this energy flows from you to the staff and students with whom you work.

Of course, the opposite is also true. Negative emotions are contagious too. Some researchers test this by planting *bad apples*—actors to manipulate a situation—in meetings to disturb the group. For example, Eugen Dimant (2019), an associate professor of practice in behavioral and decision sciences at the University of Pennsylvania, finds that just one person can have a huge impact on how others in the group feel and how successful the group results are. I suspect your own experiences back this up. How well do you work when you are irritated, hurt, or angry? Have you seen one angry person derail a meeting and the impacts of that on your colleagues?

Over time, and if not addressed, that rolling snowball just gets bigger, and the result is lower attendance, higher stress levels, lower productivity, and the extremely dangerous *presenteeism*—the lost productivity that occurs when employees are not fully functioning in the workplace because of an illness, injury, or other condition (Lohaus & Habermann, 2019). In education, it could be the teacher who closes the classroom door and treats the classroom like an island. It could be the custodian just putting in time and the bare minimum of unenthusiastic effort until the end of a shift because no one cares anyway. It could be the principal avoiding difficult conversations or finding reasons to be out of the building.

Often, presenteeism is when a person intentionally withdraws from anything social or extra because the person doesn't feel valued. This person thinks things like, "Forget it. I worked hard, I gave up countless volunteer hours, and no one appreciated me, so I am only going to do what I have to now." Sometimes presenteeism is obvious, and people will say these things aloud or clearly communicate their thoughts via crossed arms or other clear body language; other times, it is more subtle. Both types of presenteeism can undermine a work culture and cost a lot in terms of lost productivity and work quality.

Have you ever talked to someone who is just waiting for retirement—or, even worse, do you know people *everyone else* is just waiting to retire or give up and transfer to another place? How productive and happy do you suppose those people are? What impact does that have on the overall culture of a school or workplace? Can you feel it? Sometimes presenteeism is not just a person putting in time, giving up, or burning out. Sometimes it is a person who comes to work but doesn't feel safe with or connected to the person's team. All the people in these examples impact one another and influence the culture of the school or workplace in one direction or another. I will discuss the impacts people have on one another's well-being more in the following chapters, but for now, the important thing to remember is *taking care of your own well-being is also taking care of the well-being of the people around you.* It is perhaps one of the greatest gifts you can give them.

The Business Case for Well-Being

From a strictly practical financial point of view, there is an important business case to make for paying attention to well-being in the workplace. If people are healthier, they come to work. A study of Ontario teachers finds investing in a positive workplace reduces teacher absenteeism by an average of five days per teacher per year (Schmidt et al., 2019). There is also a cost to people coming to work when they are unwell. If someone is physically at work but unwell, it can impact the person's productivity and quality of work. The estimated costs of presenteeism are somewhere between four-and-a-half and seven-and-a-half days per employee per year (Schmidt et al., 2019).

However, a study of Canadian companies finds that every dollar spent on having a comprehensive well-being strategy over three years saves $2.18 (in Canadian dollars) on health-related human resources costs (Deloitte Insights, 2019). EdCan Network (n.d.) reported the following figures relating to educator stress and burnout.

- 58 percent of K–12 teachers are stressed "all the time" compared with 36 percent of the overall Canadian workforce.
- 40 percent report that they are not coping well with their job stress.
- 85 percent feel this is affecting their ability to teach.

Schools that invested in K–12 workplace well-being found that:

- Teachers reported five fewer absences per year
- Increased teacher well-being correlated with increased student achievement
- Increased teacher well-being correlated with increasingly supportive teacher-student relationships

This document (EdCan Network, n.d.) is a fantastic resource to share with decision makers or partner groups when you want to make the business case for education staff well-being. The numbers are compelling and clear: it is expensive to have educators who are unwell.

Beyond the actual financial cost, think about what happens to the rest of the system when there is high absenteeism, presenteeism, and burnout. Have you been that principal with two or three classes in the gym because you don't have enough coverage for classes? Many principals spend every morning doing the coverage "shuffle." What does that do to the principal's relationships with staff members, and the principal's own job satisfaction and well-being? Consider the following example.

> Every morning at 5:00 a.m., Tracy, an elementary school principal, checks the absence list to help prepare herself for what the day may hold. At 6:30 a.m., when she is already at work and the callout for substitute teachers happens, she checks every five minutes or so to see if the positions are filled. Many times all absences are filled by 8:00 a.m., but sometimes they are not, and then she must figure out what to do next. Does she cover the class or classes herself and get behind on everything else? She does love the chance to connect with the students, but there are two parents already waiting to

talk to her, and they don't look happy! Does she ask one of her non-enrolling teachers (such as a learning assistance or resource teacher) again and take that support away from students who need it? She knows the resource teacher will do it because she is always so helpful, but maybe she should ask someone different this time, even if that teacher won't be too happy? She can't help but feel frustrated that the teacher she and her staff are replacing is away a lot, particularly at report card time. Tracy is trying not to let that thought irritate her or impact the relationship with the teacher who is away, and wonders if other staff members are feeling that way too.

This is how Tracy's day starts before she even leaves home in the morning. As she walks out the door, she asks her partner if she can retire yet. Her partner laughs and says, "Not yet; go to work!" and they both smile, but it is not really a joke. Tracy would retire in a heartbeat if she could.

The business case for well-being is already compelling, but Tracy's story reminds leaders that well-being also has a personal and relational cost; the benefits of well-being have an exponential impact on the entire system.

The Bottom Line

Researchers, and indeed your own experiences, provide you with some truly scary statistics and stories of how stress and burnout can impact a school. It is important to know how higher levels of stress impact your health, happiness, and success as an individual and as an education system. Fortunately, the practices that move people toward well-being are not difficult, and they are also contagious. These strategies require awareness, intention, and practice. There are simple and beautiful practices individuals or teams can do together. There are also ways to support well-being at a systems level, and I will discuss those ways in the following chapters.

Ultimately, paying attention to well-being can have a tremendous impact on schools and other workplaces and the people in them. Everyone deserves to work in a place that allows them to grow and contribute. Everyone deserves to be happy and healthy. That is what parents want for their children as they grow up, and it is what education leaders need and deserve in their own lives too.

Well-Being Action Steps

1. Take the business case for well-being to financial leaders and decision makers.

2. Find out what is going on in your own district or community about absenteeism, retention, and stress-related leaves of absence.

3. Start a conversation about presenteeism and engagement.

4. Pay attention to your own engagement and what parts of your job give or deplete your energy.

5. Seek out and review local, state or provincial, or national standards for psychological well-being in the workplace and compare them to your school's work environment. For example, if you live in Canada, review the National Standard website (https://scc.ca/en/agl-nsc) and documents from the Mental Health Commission of Canada (n.d.) to find out if your workplace is using these guidelines. Even if you cannot locate guidelines specific to your geographic location, guidelines such as these can be helpful!

The *Self*
The Beauty of and Problems With Self-Care

> Awareness is the greatest agent for change.
> —Eckhart Tolle

I believe in the power of self-care, and I believe people are each responsible for taking care of their own health and well-being. However, I also want to warn you that leaders, even those trying to best support their teams, can sometimes get this practice wrong. When leaders get it wrong, then well-intentioned, well-supported self-care programs can inadvertently do more harm than good. When leaders do it well, then supporting self-care strategies and practices can make a significant difference in staff lives. Practicing and supporting self-care are essential components of an effective workplace well-being plan and a particularly valuable place to start.

In this chapter, I will discuss the traditional approach to self-care, including the ways in which this historical approach is akin to putting an adhesive bandage on an elephant-sized problem. Leaders will then discover ways to appropriately share effective self-care practices before discussing the importance of self-awareness to well-being. The chapter concludes with a list of self-care action steps you can begin implementing right away.

THE TRADITIONAL APPROACH TO SELF-CARE

Traditional workplace wellness programs are often more about handling and supporting workplace illness than about creating well-being. These programs involve things like providing mental health for stress leaves when necessary and then return-to-work supports to help employees successfully transition back to work. These are much-needed and appreciated supports for people who are struggling with illness of any kind. The part that human resources practices traditionally fail to consider is the *prevention and promotion* parts of self-care. How do leaders support well-being, prevent burnout, and decrease or prevent the need for stress leaves in the first place?

There has been some movement toward prevention with attendance support programs, but these programs typically only target certain groups of employees and can be seen (indeed, they are sometimes run) as being more punitive than supportive. For example, all teachers in one school district were sent a letter telling them attendance had been low on Black Friday, a popular shopping day on the Friday after Thanksgiving in the United States. The email reminded educators that leaders expect them to report to work that day and also discussed the consequences of non-attendance.

Take a moment to imagine receiving that email, and think about what such a message might do to the relationships between the school district leaders and their employees. The employees who would *not* miss work to go shopping—the huge majority—would potentially feel annoyed at being told something so obvious. The few who would have missed may work on that day in the future but are no less likely to miss work on other days. Further, it's a big assumption to presume all people absent are, quite literally, skipping school, and those who are absent for genuine reasons may feel like leadership is treating them poorly for taking a valid day off. While a leader might review such absences case-by-case so as not to treat everyone as irresponsible and in need of a lecture, the key takeaway is that even the most supportive attendance-management program still only supports the population of employees who miss work consistently. The program does not help the employees who may be struggling and unwell but still come to work.

When human resources departments lead health promotion, some of the often-used strategies are to provide employees with information through newsletters, emails, or video campaigns regarding ways to take care of themselves. Traditionally, this health information includes physical health strategies like maintaining proper nutrition, getting enough exercise, and understanding the importance of sleep, among other excellent health information. More effective approaches treat this information as holistic, providing people with information and strategies about things like stress management, positive psychology, and other social, emotional, mental, and even spiritual health topics. In this way, leaders acknowledge and value the interconnected parts of health. For example, many employee-assistance plans have self-care articles and tips about resilience, relaxation techniques, and practicing gratitude. Including these positive psychology tips and strategies is an important move toward the promotion of well-being, but there is still one dangerous pitfall leaders need to know about and avoid as they promote and support self-care: *individual self-care is not enough.*

THE BANDAGE ON THE ELEPHANT

As a leader, are you reading this chapter on self-care and thinking about how you can support your staff to look after their health? Instead, think for a minute about your own health and self-care strategies. How would you feel if, in the next few paragraphs, I laid out some plans and ideas for you to increase your exercise, eat healthier, and practice breathing exercises? What if I also explained how doing these things regularly would improve your well-being and make things much better in your schools and workplaces?

Some of you would think, "Bring it on. I would love some tips on how to be healthy!" However, some of you would find this annoying. You know these plans are important, but with the increasing demands on your time and all the new mandates you must implement, you likely don't have time to put them into practice. Reading more about what you already know is an issue, but when you don't have time to apply that knowledge, it feels like a colossal waste of time, not to mention proof that I totally don't understand you.

"We are learning completely new systems and how to work in masks [due to COVID-19 restrictions] and in cohort groups. Everything is upside down, and classroom teachers are reporting a lot of stress. My colleagues and I can't connect and collaborate in the same way, and we are missing that too. We are finding ways to make it work, but at the end of the day, teachers are feeling a whole new level of exhaustion. I know the intention is good, but when that wellness email invades my inbox every week, I just want to scream!"

—Secondary teacher (personal communication, January 2021)

You are likely familiar with the phrase *the elephant in the room*, which refers to a big, obvious problem or factor everyone is aware of but no one acknowledges. Well, if the room is the education workplace, an elephant in that room is the stress and burnout educators experience there. Educators know they face a battle with stress and burnout, but few mention it or want to discuss it. And putting a finger-length bandage (individual self-care tips) on an elephant (stress and burnout) won't make it leave the room (workplace).

Leaders must be incredibly careful that making productive health decisions or practicing self-care does not become a character issue. Again, people work in complex systems, and individuals are responsible for their own health—to a certain extent. If I'm a teacher on your staff, your goal isn't to guilt me into action or take personal responsibility for my individual health. However, many things are the responsibility of the collective or institution outside the individual's control. As a leader, you cannot *only* focus on what the individual (self) is doing. You must also acknowledge that *how your staff work together* (other) and *how your system is structured* (system) also have an impact. Recognizing and acting on the self, other, *and* system components of self-care will get that elephant moving in the right direction: out of the room.

> *The education workplace is a complex system, so leaders must be careful to acknowledge that and make sure self-care support is not used as—or even seen as—a bandage-on-an-elephant solution.*

Ways to Share Effective Self-Care Practices

It is important for everyone to learn about the powerful health benefits of self-care, so how do leaders spread the word about effective self-care practices without making self-care look like an inadequate adhesive bandage? I suggest three simple steps, which I explain in detail in the following sections.

1. Acknowledge that self-care is just one part of a larger plan.
2. Keep messages simple and personal.
3. Include SEL in SELf-care.

Acknowledge That Self-Care Is Just One Part of a Larger Plan

While supporting self-care among your staff, acknowledge and create a placeholder for the other parts of well-being—wellness of others and wellness within the organizational system, as figure I.1 (page 5) illustrates—even if you are not working on those other parts yet. Even just mentioning there are three parts and which ones you are working on helps frame the work and lets people know you know the importance of considering all three interconnected parts.

For example, I worked with a district leader who put together an excellent presentation on staff well-being. We met as a district team to develop the presentation that team members would then share with school-level teams. The team was only at the beginning of a journey into developing a staff well-being plan and was focused more on traditional self-care support and also on building team relationships and connections. The team knew this was a great place to start, and members knew they needed to act immediately, but they also wanted to acknowledge they knew work was needed at the systems level. The team wanted to both hear from school staff and reassure them support was available.

There was a small amount of money schools could apply for to support well-being, with little required in return other than a short report about what the school used the money for. The report the team needed to file (see figure 2.1, page 28) simply allowed the district to see what each school team was doing so members could share the ideas and get some feedback about what worked well. My team added three checkboxes to the short report form so school teams could report if they used their money to support individual self-care, collective care for one another, or some kind of system support or change. There was no pressure for school teams to do anything in particular, nor was it their responsibility to do it all, but each school had the opportunity to be creative and do what worked for its staff. Just having the three boxes on the form was both an acknowledgment and an excellent prompt to expand people's understanding of well-being. This concept is so simple, you could easily use a form like figure 2.1 for your district or school.

A form like the one in figure 2.1 prepares school teams with a great mix of empathy and acknowledgment of the challenges. The presentation should include a list of existing resources staff can access, like counseling available through an employee-assistance program, union-sponsored web-based stress-management programs, and other links for more health information. Note that this approach still embodies a traditional approach to promoting information about well-being. There is still a need to provide information about where to go for support, but such an offering must include an acknowledgment that well-being is bigger than just looking after oneself. It's critical to include a slide or handout page about the three interconnected parts of well-being (self, other, and system). When our district team did this, I could almost hear the sigh of relief when staff saw it was not all their responsibility to make things better.

Although our presentation and the well-being supports we offered were both wonderful strategies, I do not share this story to imply you should adopt these specific strategies exactly as we did, but rather to emphasize that no matter what

There are *three* parts that work together to promote our well-being.
We have to consider them all together.

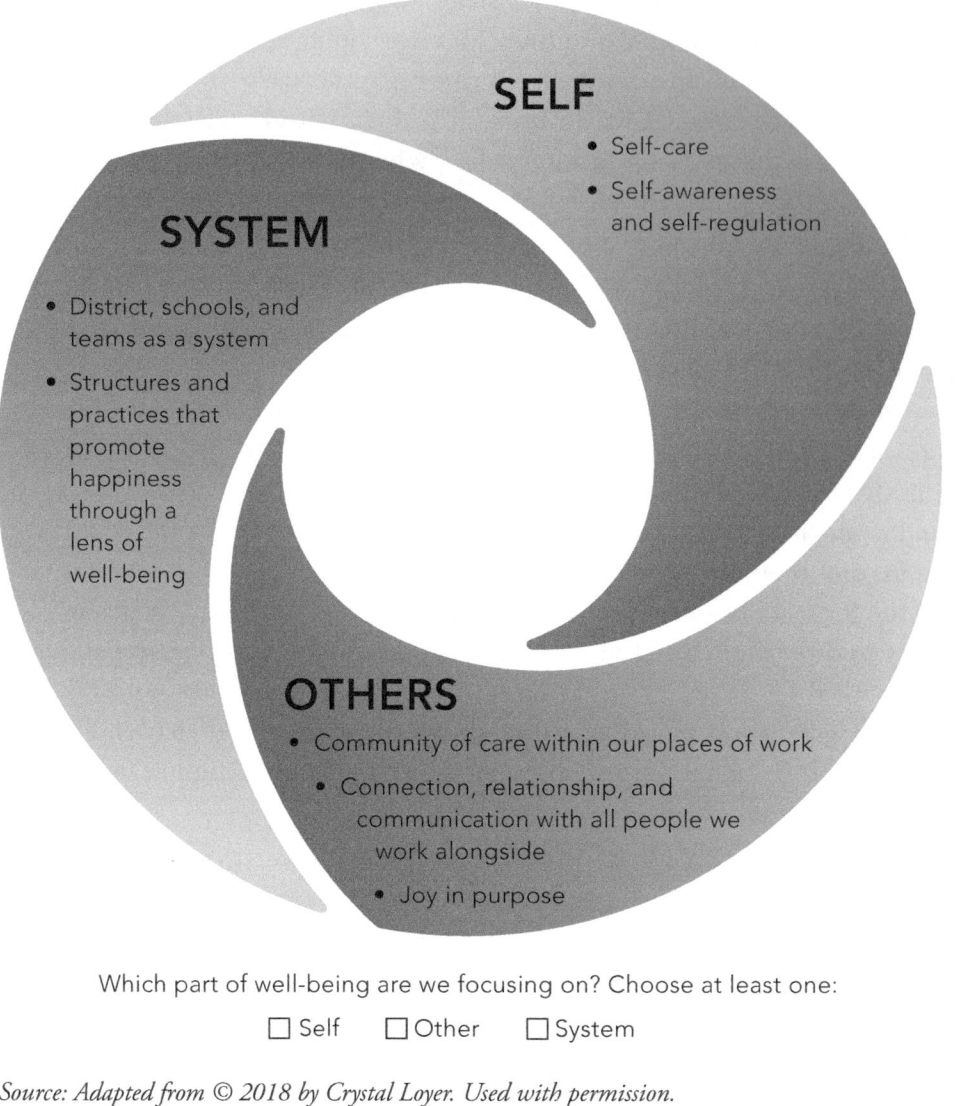

Which part of well-being are we focusing on? Choose at least one:
☐ Self ☐ Other ☐ System

Source: Adapted from © 2018 by Crystal Loyer. Used with permission.

Figure 2.1: Example of ways to acknowledge all three parts of well-being.
*Visit **go.SolutionTree.com/educatorwellness** for a free reproducible version of this figure.*

self-care support and suggestions you offer, please remember to *acknowledge* to staff that individual self-care is just one part of the plan. Self-care is an important part of well-being, but it is not sufficient all by itself. In other words, let your employees know you see the elephant!

Keep Messages Simple and Personal

Very few people want long, detailed messages about self-care practices filling up their already-full inboxes. If you have ever struggled with an overflowing inbox, you know receiving emails you didn't ask for that suggest you do something you don't have time for is not benign or neutral. There is nothing wrong with providing links to additional details in your messages for anyone who wants to learn more about a particular point or topic, but be thoughtful about the length and frequency of the messages you do send out.

The Behavioural Insights Team (https://bi.team), which studied effective communication during COVID-19 in England and North America, finds it is very important to simplify communication to reduce employees' cognitive load when things get overwhelming (as cited in Larson & Jivapong, 2021). Present the most important facts first, use as few words as possible, and do not worry about fancy design or pictures; some of the most effective messages are pictureless. In the same study, coauthors Emily Larson and Belinda Jivapong (2021) also find that health messages are more impactful when a trusted leader or influencer (at any level of the organization) delivers them, rather than a human resources representative employees don't know well.

Another study from the Behavioral Insights Team invited principals to send weekly text messages or emails to their staff (as cited in EdCan Network, 2021). The messages came from four evidence-based concept areas proven to increase well-being: (1) well-being endorsement, (2) *fresh start* (the energy for wiping the slate clean and starting again), (3) mental health support during COVID-19, and (4) gratitude (as cited in EdCan Network, 2021). The researchers gave the principals a list of short, simple, prewritten messages to choose from and encouraged them to make the messages their own. Principals reported positive responses from the prewritten emails when they took the time to adapt the messages to their own school culture (as cited in EdCan Network, 2021). Additionally, the recipients reported enjoying the messages coming directly from their leaders and noted the messages served as a reminder to focus on their own well-being (as cited in EdCan Network, 2021). You can easily adapt prewritten evidence-based text messages or emails to fit your school or work team's own context and provide the benefit of an easy-to-implement strategy while maintaining a personal, authentic message.

Include SEL in SELf-Care

If you really want to harness the power of self-care, move beyond the traditional health promotion materials and include social-emotional learning (SEL) practices. All staff, including leaders, still need health reminders, so keep sending those important messages and opportunities. However, moving beyond promotional materials and reminders to practicing and embedding SEL skills in the workplace has a much stronger impact on overall well-being and workplace success (Schonert-Reichl, 2017; Wisniewski & Foster, 2020). The same advantages students get from having these skills also apply to adults, so practicing them yourself helps your own well-being and has the added bonus of making you and your staff better models for your students (Wisniewski & Foster, 2020).

Recall the five CASEL competencies in chapter 1 (page 9). Notice the two parts of the circle that relate to the individual are *self-awareness* and *self-management* (self-regulation). In her book *Insight: Why We're Not as Self-Aware as We Think, and How Seeing Ourselves Clearly Helps Us Succeed at Work and in Life*, Tasha Eurich (2017), an organizational psychologist, researcher, and best-selling author, calls *self-awareness* the "meta-skill of the 21st century" because this skill underlies and supports the skills important for success (like communication, collaboration, empathy, connection, and so on; p. 5). Eurich (2017) also notes, "Self-awareness is, at its core, the ability to see ourselves clearly—to understand who we are, how others see us, and how we fit into the world" (p. 3).

Happily, this impactful, primary SEL skill is not difficult and doesn't take a lot of time—just some intention, practice, and a willingness to be open to the sometimes difficult practice of learning about yourself.

Self-Care Begins With Being Self-Aware

Are you self-aware? If I asked you to measure your level of self-awareness on a scale of 1–5, what would you give yourself? I am going to guess you would rate yourself as above average on self-awareness because if you are reading this book, you are probably an educator and a leader. Educators and leaders are generally more self-aware people, right? After all, these are the skills they teach. Well, unfortunately, that assumption is inaccurate. Eurich (2017) says approximately 90 percent of people rate their self-awareness above average, but it turns out self-awareness is actually not predictable by occupation, education level, gender, ethnicity, or any of the usual demographic information.

Other researchers confirm Eurich's (2017) finding that people are not as self-aware as they think they are. A meta-analysis of studies that compared people's self-assessment of their abilities and performances shows only a moderate connection between how people *thought* they did and actual performance outcomes (Zell & Križan, 2014). In reality, only 10 to 15 percent of people are actually accurate predictors of their performance level. Think about people who fall outside this category—people who think they are very self-aware but have no idea they do not come across in the same way. This discrepancy is likely because there are actually two parts to self-awareness: (1) internal and (2) external (Eurich, 2019).

Internal Self-Awareness Practices

Internal self-awareness involves being aware of your feelings and thoughts and how they impact you and your interactions with the world. It is about understanding your values, what your passions or interests are, and your usual patterns and reactions (Eurich, 2019). People who are skilled at internal self-awareness have a sense of who they are and what they want, and they lead happier and more successful lives because of it. Having an awareness of your own feelings and thoughts and how those feelings impact your behavior gives you more control over the way you interact with the world, making your interactions more successful, which also contributes to more positive emotions (Eurich, 2019).

Two internal self-awareness practices you may like to try to improve your own self-awareness are (1) notice, label, act, and (2) the ladder of inference.

Notice, Label, Act

Internal self-awareness is about slowing things down enough to notice what is going on inside so you can act with intention. The first thing to do is notice where you experience feelings in your body. Do you feel a tightness in your chest, like me, or do you feel butterflies or something more sinister in your stomach? You may have multiple answers, and that's fine—you can notice many, but most people have one or two prominent sensations. If you are working on developing or improving internal self-awareness, recognizing feelings in your body is the place to start. It sounds simple, and it is, but don't underestimate the power of just noticing and being curious about your physical responses because feelings always start in the body. Instead of treating feelings as unimportant or a nuisance in daily life, try thinking of feelings as important information, because how you feel impacts your thoughts and behavior (whether you acknowledge these feelings or not). Noticing your reactions is the best way to start the process of integrating and regulating your feelings, thoughts, and actions so they work together in a way that supports your values and intentions.

For some, this is easy. However, if you were taught to hide or ignore feelings, or if it wasn't safe for you to express feelings when you were a child, this step may be new to you, so be patient with yourself. Watch out for your own judgments about how you react to stimuli, and let these judgments go. In his book *Permission to Feel*, Marc Brackett (2020), a research psychologist and founding director of the Yale Center for Emotional Intelligence and a professor in the Child Study Center at Yale University, writes that feelings are data, not directives. Feelings are not in charge of how you act, but it is dangerous to ignore them. Just like the stress response, ignored feelings don't just vanish on their own but "pile up like a debt that will eventually come due" (Brackett, 2020, p. 13).

So once you notice and are curious about whatever is happening in your body, you will probably be able to put a label on what you feel. The human brain has a tendency to keep things simple, and the average adult describes his or her feelings using surprisingly few words. Yet, accurately labeling your emotions helps you move toward more effective solutions, communicates your needs better, and physically calms the brain and body (Burklund, Creswell, Irwin, & Lieberman, 2014).

Once you have some awareness of what is going on and have labeled your feelings in some way, you can decide what to do about your feelings and their underlying causes. There are three action options: (1) lean in, (2) let go, or (3) solve the problem.

1. **Lean in:** This action is for the good feelings that fill your soul. When you notice one of those feelings, lean in! Take a minute or two to hold on to that good feeling and really experience it. It is powerful if you can talk about it and share it with others, but even if you don't have time in that moment, take a quick mental snapshot and go back to it later. You can always go back and think about that moment, revisit the feeling, and get the health benefits that positive feelings provide. Positive visualizations release similar brain chemicals as the actual event (more about that in chapter 3, page 45) and have similar physical results, such as strengthening your immune systems and promoting faster healing (Sheerha & Singhvi, 2016). Try it right now for a minute, and you will see what I am talking about. Think about a time when a student, staff member, or colleague thanked you for something or told you about a positive impact you had on them. Close your eyes for a minute and remember it. Where were you, and what did that moment look, smell, and feel like? Smile as you visualize the scene and hear the person's words. Have a few of these visualizations ready in your back pocket when you need them.

2. **Let go:** The beauty of self-awareness is that noticing and labeling an emotion slow you down just long enough to think it through a bit. Consider whether your reaction is in line with your values, beliefs, and desires. If it isn't, consciously allow that feeling to leave your body. You could do this with a change in self-talk, a few deep breaths, your favorite exercise after work, a talk with a friend, or whatever works for you to move that feeling out of your brain and body. There are many options

for regulating emotions and completing the stress response cycle, but the important part is noticing it is happening without judgment (having feelings is normal!) and finding out which strategies work best for you. Try them out until you have a list of a few strategies that work for you in different situations. (The reproducible "Steps to Build and Use Self-Awareness" on page 41 will help you identify these strategies.) You may find taking a long run is great for you, but you can't do that in the middle of a staff meeting or every time you feel irritated, so you need a few options to choose from.

3. **Solve the problem:** This option is about engaging in an action to address whatever has created the emotional response or at least investigate it in some way. One opportune time to use this strategy is after you try the let go approach and it's not working (although solving the problem may also be the very first strategy you try!). You will know because the undesirable feeling will keep happening. Whether you are addressing a problem in the moment or returning to something you are having trouble letting go of, this is an excellent time to start with important feelings data, so you can do some problem solving. (See page 41 for the reproducible, "Steps to Build and Use Self-Awareness.")

Here is an example of putting these steps into practice. Imagine your colleague has made a comment about her latest blog post, and you notice your shoulders tense up. You know her weekly blog post is amazing, and you have tried to write a blog as well, but you never really have time to get to it. Now what?

First, take a quick moment to be impressed that you noticed your emotion instead of letting it out as irritation with her or with some other innocent person who happens by. You don't have to do anything with the emotion at first—just notice it and be curious. If you are new to this process, stop there for now. Just practice noticing for a while. After you get good at noticing, the next step is labeling. Are you jealous? Irritated? Impressed? You can have all those feelings at the same time, so don't worry too much about the label except to give the emotion you feel one (or several). Once you label the feelings, they are no longer in charge; you get to decide what to do with them. You may decide you are jealous about your colleague's blog post. She manages to do so many things and makes everything look amazing and easy, which you find really irritating!

After labeling comes the need to act, either letting go or solving the problem. Making this determination depends on the nature of the problem and where your personal values lie. In *EMPOWER Moves for Social-Emotional Learning*, veteran educator Lauren Porosoff and clinical psychologist and mental health expert

Jonathan Weinstein (2023) describe four features of values: (1) they are a consequence of your experiences, (2) they are freely chosen, (3) they are different from preferences, and (4) they are qualities of action. Being mindful of acting in accordance with your values can guide your actions. For example, perhaps one of your values is connection, and you really want to be a colleague who celebrates and learns from others instead of competing. After noticing your reaction and reminding yourself about this value, you may decide to choose to let go of the irritation and jealousy. Since you are at work, you take a few deep breaths—a strategy you are well-practiced in—until you feel the tension in your shoulders dissipate. Within a few minutes, you notice your well-being has markedly improved.

The Ladder of Inference

It is important to note that although your feelings are excellent sources of data to pay attention to, the stories your brain puts together to explain them are often inaccurate (Brown, 2018). For example, maybe the story your brain tells is your colleague's blog posts about teaching successes are only so exceptional because she keeps getting placed at well-funded schools, which lack severe systemic challenges that inhibit teaching and learning. Your brain tells you school leaders are grooming her for promotion and giving her all the best opportunities, when the reality of their motivation might be much different. Your brain is prone to drawing inaccurate conclusions, but this is not through any fault of your own; rather, the outside world provides your brain with too much data for you to take in, so your brain selects some of the data (based on your previous experiences) and constructs these data into a story. Your brain rewards you not for accuracy, but for completing the story (Burton, 2013).

An excellent tool individuals and teams can use to discover their tendencies surrounding these stories is the *ladder of inference*. Chris Argyris (1990), an American business theorist and professor emeritus at Harvard Business School, originally developed the ladder of inference, a well-used tool in the Compassionate Systems Leadership work of Peter Senge and colleagues (2012) at the Center for Systems Awareness (https://systemsawareness.org). This model helps people understand how often they make assumptions based on their own experiences and worldviews, instead of the more objective facts of the situation (Fiester, 2022). The ladder, as figure 2.2 shows, involves seven stages in story-building—(1) available data, (2) selected data, (3) interpretations, (4) assumptions, (5) conclusions, (6) beliefs, and (7) actions—that lead to either a *jumping to conclusions* outcome or a *reflective* outcome. To use the ladder template, stop and question your reasoning at each rung of the ladder by asking questions such as the following.

Source: Adapted from Amran, 2022.

Figure 2.2: Ladder of inference questions.

The ladder helps you slow down your reactions so you can question your assumptions and respond to situations with more intention. The ability to notice your own tendencies to move up and down the ladder and to slow down your meaning-making process with intention makes the ladder an excellent self-awareness tool. It is also helpful to use the ladder collaboratively with colleagues to increase communication, level of trust, and resilience among team members (Schlegel & Parascando, 2020); I discuss this in more detail in chapter 4 (page 71).

Here's an example of how the ladder of inference helped an elementary school principal slow down her reactions and act with intention at her new school.

> *Deanna, an elementary school principal, uses the ladder of inference for herself and as an exercise with her team to help everyone be more aware of the fact that an initial understanding of or reaction to something isn't the only possibility. Deanna's job, for example, is full of quick decisions and reactions, and most of the time, she likes that part of the job. But now, she has begun to recognize a familiar sick feeling in her stomach when faced with a difficult decision. This feeling reminds her to stop and slow it down a bit or go back to it.*

> Earlier that week, Deanna was leading a staff meeting at her new school and trying to connect with the staff. The staff did some great exercises to build up the team, but at every opportunity, some people were on their devices. Deanna tried to ignore this behavior and focus on the day, but it was distracting. She had so many thoughts about it: it was rude, the staff members were clearly uninterested, and she felt a need to take control of the situation quickly. Then, she thought about the ladder and realized she could be making assumptions and drawing conclusions that may not even be true. Maybe those things were true, but maybe they weren't. Deanna took a moment to regroup and then address the issue in a much better way than she might have without this moment of self-reflection. That is all it took. Just that brief moment made a huge difference in how she felt and acted during the rest of the meeting.
>
> At the beginning of the next staff meeting, Deanna had a conversation with her new team and told members about her experience. She talked about how the ladder helped her rethink the situation. The conversation allowed her to have an authentic conversation about how she was feeling, the opportunity to introduce the tool, and the chance to problem solve the issue of device use in meetings.

Look at figure 2.3 to see how you might utilize the ladder of inference to solve a challenge similar to what Deanna faced.

Try using the ladder of inference form in figure 2.3 to work through one of your own school-based situations. You can find a blank version of this form at **go.SolutionTree.com/educatorwellness**.

The ladder of inference is only a tool, of course. The important thing here is to slow down the process and be aware of your own assumptions. A tool isn't required for that, but it can help support your efforts or the efforts of staff members. Another important thing to remember is you can move up and down the ladder and make assumptions and decisions all day, and you do that really quickly, which is usually an exceptionally positive thing. It keeps you moving forward and getting things done. That is why you must pay attention to the feelings cues that tell you something different is going on. Those are the data you want to pay attention to if you want to harness the power of internal self-awareness. It sounds like a lot of steps, but it really takes only a few extra minutes and saves so much time in the end. Remember, it is a practice, so go one step at a time and be patient with yourself.

External Self-Awareness Practices

After you have practiced paying attention to your own thoughts, feelings, and behaviors, it is a good idea to check out how other people experience you. Are you

	Examples From Deanna's Story	
Ladder of Inference Steps	**Jumping to Conclusions Option**	**Reflective Option**
7. Actions You take actions based on your prior beliefs and conclusions.	I'm not going to allow any more devices at staff meetings.	I'm going to hold a conversation about how we work together and circle back to check my assumptions. I now have an excellent example to share!
6. Beliefs You draw conclusions based on facts you interpret and your prior assumptions.	These staff are not working together, and clearly I have been put here to fix a broken system. I need to reset some boundaries and rules about staff meeting behavior.	There are some things we need to talk about as a team to make communication and practices clearer.
5. Conclusions You draw conclusions based on your prior beliefs.	I need to get things under control and refocus the meeting as this is not a cohesive team. The staff don't want me here.	The staff may not want me to be here, but there are many other possibilities too. I can leverage the engagement happening to create even more engagement.
4. Assumptions You make assumptions based on the meaning you give to your observations.	This behavior is rude and disrespectful. The staff are not listening to me, and things are getting out of my control.	I am assuming the staff are distracted because that is what happens to me when I am on a device in meetings. This may not be the same for everyone. How do I know they are not listening?
3. Interpretations You interpret facts and give them a personal meaning.	These devices are distracting staff, and they are not participating in the meeting.	There is engagement in the meeting. Staff could be taking notes or engaging with the meeting on their devices.
2. Selected Data You select facts based on your convictions and prior experiences.	I am leading a staff meeting. Some people are on devices.	Some people are not on devices. Staff were talking and connecting before the meeting. Some people are giving input.
1. Available Data You observe information from the real world.	Approximately thirty staff members are present in a staff meeting, seated in four rows in front of me. The room is well lit with natural light, and a slight breeze is blowing through the open windows at the side of the room. A moderate degree of ambient noise is present outside the windows as students leave school for the day and shout to one another. Some staff members are talking quietly in the meeting room. There are a couple of computers open on tables in front of some staff members, and three people are typing into phones.	

Figure 2.3: Using the ladder of inference example.

Visit **go.SolutionTree.com/educatorwellness** *for a free blank reproducible version of this figure.*

aware of how you come across to others? Most tests of self-awareness are self-report measures, but what if you also asked other people to answer the same questions?

In doing the research for this book, I did a self-awareness quiz that required not only my responses but also those of a trusted friend before offering a score (The Eurich Group, 2022). I asked my husband and apparently, I should have asked someone else because he got it all wrong! We have been married for over thirty years, and he sees me differently than I see myself. What was going on?

It turns out there are two equally important parts of self-awareness, and even though I had been teaching and practicing *internal* self-awareness, I needed to become more curious and seek feedback on *external* self-awareness (or how others see me). Research shows people who know how others perceive them are more skilled at taking the perspective of others (Eurich, 2019). When leaders can show they have knowledge of how others experience them, others see them as more trustworthy and effective. Employees report they are more satisfied working with and for these leaders (Eurich, 2019). This makes sense because, for example, leaders who are aware they have an unconscious tendency to come across as too direct and task-focused can first make a conscious effort to ask questions more and connect more with the people doing the task. This bit of awareness of how others perceive them allows leaders to make changes that support their relationships with others and ultimately get the task done more successfully.

So, how do you find out how you come across to others? The simple answer, of course, is to ask them, but do this thoughtfully. You need someone who cares about you and wants the best for you but who is also able to give you clear and honest feedback. Feedback is particularly important for leaders to seek out, but it is often difficult because leaders know fewer people who will give them the real, honest truth (Detert & Bruno, 2021). Thus, it is difficult for leaders to get a good sense of how others perceive them (Detert & Bruno, 2021).

Kristi Hedges (2019), a leadership coach and faculty member at Georgetown University, shares some simple questions to ask in her chapter of the *Harvard Business Review's* book on self-awareness. She suggests you set face-to-face meetings with a few of these key people, letting them know you would really like honest, clear feedback, and ask just two questions (Hedges, 2019):

1. What's the general perception of me?
2. What could I do differently that would have the greatest impact on my success?

Be careful to manage your reactions to these questions, as it is normal to feel defensive. Instead of reacting defensively, try to stay in a place of curiosity and remember this is not easy for the person giving feedback either. After you speak to a few people, you will begin to see patterns that may be surprising, but these patterns will give you a sense of how others see you. If what they see is what you intend, great! If your goals and their perceptions don't align, you now have a great place to start to move things into alignment.

In my own case, I learned a lot of things from asking these questions; I realized my passion for this work was often coming across to others as intense. This can put people off, put pressure on them, or both. That has never been my intention at all, and it was a little difficult to hear, but it was helpful. I decided I am not going to stop being passionate about workplace well-being, but I am going to be careful to let others know that just because I am excited about something, it doesn't mean I expect long-standing workplace culture to change overnight or others to fix issues for me. I ensure that I convey my excitement about ideas, possibilities, and opportunities to find creative solutions together.

You will probably also find useful information about yourself by doing this, but remember to be open to thinking about what these people are brave enough to tell you and compassionate to yourself as well. There will be more about receiving feedback in chapter 4 (page 71), which deals with psychological safety, but for now, as you work on self-awareness, remember to start with the people who care about you and will give you the truth from that caring space. It is a really great place to start and will make it easier when you need to expand that feedback circle later. Feedback is not always easy to hear, but if you can gain an understanding of how others perceive you and align their answers to how you want them to perceive you, think of how powerful that would be! (See page 44 for the reproducible, "Steps to Build External Self-Awareness.")

THE BOTTOM LINE

Now you have some ideas about how to promote and support self-care in general, and some specific ideas about how to include the essential social-emotional components (SELf-care) through increasing your own self-awareness and modeling this practice for others. Practicing self-awareness is a perfect connection to the next part of well-being because your own feelings, thoughts, and behaviors are all connected, but they also always occur in relationships. I examine this second aspect of well-being—*other*—in chapter 3 (page 45).

Self-Care Action Steps

1. Situate health promotion information and self-care ideas within the larger well-being framework by including all three parts of well-being in conversations and materials.

2. Keep self-care reminders short, simple, and personal. Here's an example text message: *Sharing laughter is a great way to connect with one another and lower the stress response. Here is something that made me laugh today:* [insert link to funny meme here].

3. Work on your own self-awareness and keep practicing. For example, *That feeling in my stomach is happening, and I notice I am thinking about all the reasons I am furious about this, but that was not how I wanted to be in this meeting. This may be a good time for a short break.*

4. Share your learning about self-awareness and what you are working on with your team, ask for feedback, and model or share what you have learned in your teams.

5. Acknowledge that self-awareness is a lifelong activity, and perfection is not the goal.

Steps to Build and Use Self-Awareness

Answer the following questions, and use the provided guidance to build and use self-awareness.

Where in my body do feelings show up?

What does it feel like?

Feeling words (try not to use *sad*, *mad*, *happy*, or *scared*):

You can just stop here for a while if you need to. There is no need to rush to a response right away. *When you are ready*, pick one of the responses on the following pages.

Lean Into the Good Stuff

Complete the following steps.

- Take a moment to enjoy.
- Talk about it so others can share.
- Go back and think about it when you need a lift sometime.

Complete the Stress Response Cycle

Completing the stress response cycle requires letting go of the things that don't serve you well. Use the following list of ideas to help you answer the prompt, *What works for me?*

- Take long, slow, deep breaths.
- Take a step outside.
- Move my body.
- Engage in compassionate self-talk ("I am OK. I am safe. Stay curious").
- Drink water.
- Make a social connection (even something as simple as smiling at someone as you walk down the hall can help).

Do Some Problem Solving

To begin, ask yourself: "Am I in a problem-solving emotional state right now?" If not, wait or go back and complete the stress response cycle. Next, answer the following questions.

What are my assumptions?

_____
_____
_____
_____

What is my intention?

_____
_____
_____
_____

Examples

I noticed that when _____ happened, I started feeling _____, and I started to jump ahead and make assumptions that may or may not be accurate. I wanted to check things out with you.

How were you feeling? What was happening for you?

_____
_____
_____
_____

Steps to Build External Self-Awareness

Use the following steps to build external self-awareness.

1. Take a quiz to get a sense of your self-awareness style. For example, you might choose The Eurich Group's (2022) Insight Quiz, available at www.insight-book.com/quiz.
2. Write down the names of two or three caring colleagues who will give clear answers to the questions in the quiz (Hedges, 2019).

_____
_____
_____

What is the general perception of me?

What could I do differently to have the greatest impact on my success?

What themes have I discovered?

How will this knowledge help me?

The *Other*
Social Connection and Belonging

> I define connection as the energy that exists between people when they feel seen, heard, and valued; when they can give and receive without judgment; and when they derive sustenance and strength from the relationship.
>
> —Brené Brown

If I told you there was something relatively simple you could do that would motivate and engage your students, colleagues, family members, and even yourself to work harder and better and to have more fun doing it, would you do it?

This question was the first line—the *hook*—designed to grab the audience's attention in my 2019 TEDx Talk called "The Secret to Health, Happiness and Success Together" (Markin, 2019). At least, it was *supposed* to be the first line, but I blew it. It makes me laugh now when I think about it because, really, who does that? Who blows the *first line*, the one you practice the most?

The rest of the talk turned out pretty well, and I knew it would. I knew it would go well not because I was an amazing presenter, but because what I was talking about really is the secret to all these measures of success people want for themselves and the people they care about. I was talking about belonging and the power of connection.

I started my reading and research on belonging and the power of connection to understand what makes people well. At the time, I worked with a small team to look at well-being in our school district. My role as a district counselor was to support teachers with the new physical health curriculum that included mental health and well-being for the first time. The other members of this newly formed team included a district principal, a human resources manager, and a representative from the local health authority. The team had just applied for and received a grant for a project on staff well-being, and it was becoming increasingly obvious that although team members wanted to help and support people to be well, all our district's programs and support mechanisms were kicking in when employees were already overwhelmed.

I remember telling my team members we didn't have anything for people who are struggling. They said we did have supports for the people who needed them, but these supports were mostly for employees to go on leave or to support employees with a gradual return from leave. It was the traditional model I outlined in chapter 2 (page 23). I told the team members we needed to be proactive and provide preventive supports, the tools that would help our teachers, administrators, and support staff *before* the burnout happens or the problems get too big.

Our district's traditional programs and available information encouraged self-care activities, but that often wasn't enough to maintain or renew employees' well-being. Imagine for a moment a person, Diane, who is not only taking rather good care of herself but is also *excellent* at self-care. Diane eats nutritious food, gets plenty of uninterrupted sleep, exercises regularly, and has a great support network of friends and family she connects with regularly. She even meditates daily.

Diane is definitely doing her part to contribute to her own well-being, but what happens if Diane does not feel like part of her team at work? What if the other members of her team don't want her there or are actively trying to get rid of her? Will she be well at work? Do you think more self-care suggestions or seeing a counselor to work on herself is going to help Diane with this issue? The problem, in this case, lies not in the self but in the other—in *relationships*—and this problem can only be solved in the context of relationships.

This chapter delves into people's biological need to belong and create connections and relationships in their workplaces as well as their external lives. It introduces belonging cues and action strategies leaders can use to increase social connection and belonging both for themselves and their team members. I then discuss ways to promote connection rather than competition, and highlight the potential challenges of negativity bias and inaccurate story creation. As with the other chapters, this chapter concludes with action steps to implement.

THE NEED TO BELONG

Human infants are born helpless and unable to take care of themselves. Because of this—and because humans are not the strongest or fastest animals on the planet—people need others to survive. To stay alive, people have evolved over millions of years to become a deeply social species. Their brains are designed to reward for connecting, and punish for anything that threatens people's relationships with others. In his book *Social: Why Our Brains Are Wired to Connect*, Matthew D. Lieberman (2013), a professor and Social Cognitive Neuroscience Lab director at the UCLA Department of Psychology, Psychiatry and Biobehavioral Sciences, notes people's need to belong is one of the primary drivers of human behavior. In studying the impacts of social cues on the brain's reward systems, he and other researchers find that "our brains crave the positive evaluation of others almost to an embarrassing degree" (Lieberman, 2013, p. 77).

Think about the power of understanding what motivates your behavior from a leadership perspective. Some often think in the workplace, salary or other extrinsic rewards motivate people, and that is true to a certain extent. But belonging and connection are even more powerful rewards that motivate people because they are based on the powerful human need to survive.

In collaboration with his wife, social psychologist Naomi Eisenberger, Lieberman and professor of psychology Kipling D. Williams (2003) conducted some fascinating research, where they looked at the biological basis of this powerful reward system. In this study, the researchers asked people to lie down in brain-imaging scanners and, while they were lying there, the research participants played a computerized ball game where they threw a ball back and forth with two other participants (Eisenberger et al., 2003). Imagine for a minute you are one of the unsuspecting student volunteers for this experiment, and you are playing this computer catch game. Then the other two characters (who you think are under the control of two other participants) stop throwing the ball to you. They throw the ball back and forth to each other, but never again to you. What the researchers found with this study was fascinating: when a person experiences rejection—or what they call *social pain*—it lights up or activates the same parts of the brain that light up when people experience physical pain. This reveals that rejection causes social pain and creates a response in people's neural processing not so different from what causes physical pain (Eisenberger & Lieberman, 2004; Lieberman, 2013).

Think about what this means for you as a school leader. If people experience social pain because a stranger stops throwing them a ball in a computer game, imagine what it feels like when someone feels social rejection or exclusion at work. How does this impact the way they show up and act at work?

At first, the brain's reaction to social pain just doesn't seem right because so many people consider physical pain as *real* pain and social pain as something less real, less serious. However, it actually makes sense from an evolutionary perspective because pain is a signal for danger, and social pain and rejection are huge threats to survival. Imagine what would happen if you were left out of the community in the early days of evolution. Social rejection meant certain death, so people's brains have evolved to experience it that way.

If I asked you to think about or tell a story about your most painful experiences, what would probably come to mind is not a story of a physical pain but the story of a time when you experienced some kind of relationship loss, such as the death of a loved one or the ending of a relationship. What is even more interesting is that if you were to talk about your experiences of physical pain, you would likely describe these experiences with words like "It really, really hurt" or "The pain was sharp" or even "excruciating," but you wouldn't actually be feeling that pain just describing it. If you were telling me the story of your broken heart, though, as you recounted the story, you would begin to feel the pain of that experience again in your body (Eisenberger, 2012). Neuroscientists now have research to support the notion that physical and social pain are not that different from one another (Hudd & Moscovitch, 2021).

Even though people don't experientially remember the memory of physical pain in their bodies, they do remember and feel the memory of social pain in their bodies (Hudd & Moscovitch, 2020). In fact, as Lieberman (2013) writes, "When we experience social pain or feel the distress of withheld social connection, we are unable to focus on much else until this need is met" (p. 300). Why would people's bodies store and focus on pain this way? Well, if you go back to the survival instinct and social connection being essential to human survival, then it starts to make a little more sense as to why people are designed this way.

When people remember emotional pain, the memory motivates them to avoid it. Having this understanding about how people's brains work should encourage you to take a critical and compassionate look at some of the practices in your workplace. The absolute best way to avoid emotional pain is to establish or re-establish social connection.

The good news is not only do people's brains and bodies motivate people to connect as a way to avoid pain, but they also provide some wonderful feel-good chemicals that encourage people to connect and work together. The following sections address two ways people's brains encourage connection: (1) mirror neurons and (2) the release of the brain chemicals, serotonin and oxytocin.

Mirror Neurons

People's brains connect and communicate all the time, whether people are aware of it or not. When people react to the pain they experience with empathy and a physical body response, they are communicating with one another. This is because of *mirror neurons*, specialized brain cells that allow people to instinctively connect with one another without even trying. These mirror neurons receive visual information from other people, and they react to this information (Mazurek & Schieber, 2019). This is why when I smile at you, you smile back, or if you are watching a sporting event on TV and someone gets a particularly painful-looking injury, you cringe. It's also why, when you witness an act of kindness, you feel good even when it doesn't directly impact you at all. Just watching it causes a release of chemicals in your brain that feels really good.

If you want to show the power of mirror neurons to your team, have members sit in pairs with one partner trying to remain neutral and unsmiling while the other partner smiles directly at the first partner. I have tried the following sequence with many groups of people, and I predict that five seconds or so into this thirty-second exercise, about 80 percent of the people will be laughing. The rest will complete the task, but will likely acknowledge it wasn't easy to do, and that is because they were fighting against their mirror neurons. Here are the steps to this activity.

1. Ask everyone to pair up and quickly choose who will be partner A and who will be partner B.
2. Tell everyone this is a quick thirty-second task that will begin when you say, "Go."
3. Say, "When I say to begin, Partner A, put the biggest, widest, most authentic smile on your face as you can while looking directly at partner B."
4. Say, "Partner B, look directly at partner A and keep a completely neutral face."
5. Say, "OK, thirty seconds . . . . And go!"

After thirty seconds, lead a discussion about the power of mirror neurons, emphasizing the power of smiling and laughter on mood and connection.

A personal example of the power of mirror neurons—and how they, in turn, affect your brain chemistry, as I'll discuss in the next section—happened once when I went through the drive-through at a coffee shop to discover the person ahead of me had paid for my coffee order, sending all sorts of good-feeling chemicals into my brain, the stranger's brain, and through the magic of mirror neurons, to the brains of others involved: the barista who poured my espresso shot, and my mom, who was sitting beside me in the car. I like to imagine there were children in the other car, learning and watching kindness in action; if there were, you can be sure their mirror neurons triggered a blast of feel-good chemicals in their developing brains as well. The kind stranger had no way of knowing we were on our way to my dad's hospice room that morning, and my coffee was still warm when we watched him peacefully take his last breath about an hour later.

I could digress here into many, many stories about my dad and all the virtue that was him, but my goal in relaying this story is to point out the impact of simple actions on brain chemistry and how people feel, and how those actions spread to others through mirror neurons. As my mom and I were living through a sad and difficult experience, this stranger provided a moment of connection and care that released chemicals in our brains and helped us feel good. It is both simple and powerful at the same time. When I teach students they have the power to alter one another's brain chemistry, they feel powerful, and you should too. It really is a bit of an underappreciated superpower.

Serotonin and Oxytocin

There are two particularly powerful *neurotransmitters* (the body's chemical messengers) you should know about as a leader. Both encourage people to work together and create a feeling of belonging. The first one is called *serotonin*. This is a happiness-producing brain chemical people's brains release when they feel the group values them. It is the feeling of pride you get when you receive approval from others. When serotonin is released into your brain, you connect and feel safe (Sinek, 2014). Serotonin release feels really good, and people want more of it (Carhart-Harris & Nutt, 2017), so serotonin encourages people to be loyal employees and inspiring leaders. It is a powerful incentive for people to work together because that approval feels so good. Serotonin is probably the reason people hold graduation and awards ceremonies instead of just sending the diploma in the mail, which would be so much easier. As the new graduates cross the stage, they feel a surge of serotonin, and so do their parents, grandparents, teachers, and all the people who were part of their journey.

Think for a minute about the graduation of someone you feel particularly proud of. How did it feel to watch this person walk across that stage? Can you feel it now when you think about it? Take a minute and imagine it. Close your eyes if it is easier, and visualize that experience. The beautiful thing about serotonin is the event doesn't have to be happening *right now* for you to get the benefit of a serotonin surge. It is that feeling—that rush of serotonin—that inspires people to support one another, and reminds people they are part of something bigger than themselves. Serotonin reinforces belonging. People can't get this feeling alone.

Here are some ways to use the power of serotonin to reinforce and build your connections with the people you work with.

- Smile at someone.
- Get outside and get moving (for example, take walking meetings).
- Complete a small act of kindness (for example, hold the door open for someone, give someone a compliment, pick up litter).
- Share stories about acts of kindness or celebrations.
- Be open with your approval (for example, tell someone what you value specifically about the person) and encourage others to do the same.
- Include someone in a decision or project and tell the person why you did.
- Think about a time when you felt approval or value or when you felt proud of something your team did, then share by talking to others about what it felt like.

The second neurotransmitter is an even more powerful motivator. It is called *oxytocin*, often referred to as the *love hormone* because it is the chemical associated with love, connection, friendship, and trust (Sinek, 2014). People's brains release oxytocin when they have physical contact and when they feel cared about by others (Marsh, Marsh, Lee, & Hurlemann, 2021). You will experience a rush of oxytocin when you see a picture of a baby or hold a baby and smell that beautiful baby-head smell (Marsh et al., 2021). You will feel the oxytocin filling you up. But what does all this warm and fuzzy stuff have to do with the workplace?

The same chemical that inspires people to care about helpless infants is a powerful motivator throughout life as it rewards and encourages people to care for and connect with one another (Sinek, 2014). This brain chemical is essential for both people's survival and success because it creates feelings of trust and belonging, which are the things people need for success in the workplace.

I remember once when I had first started speaking publicly and was invited to be on a panel of presenters. I was nervous and unsure why I had agreed to do this, when my boss, who had been driving through an unexpected snowstorm to get to the venue, arrived just before the event started, gave me a big hug, and whispered in my ear, "You've got this." This may sound silly, but in that moment, I felt this surge of confidence and love flood through my body, and I felt like I could do anything! I was feeling the effect of oxytocin flooding my system, but that only happened because I was fortunate to have the support of a really superb leader.

Have you ever had a friend, colleague, or boss you would do anything for? If you have, and you are thinking about that person right now, I suspect your brain is already shooting out oxytocin. Can you feel your heart filling up? Here are some ways to use the power of oxytocin to inspire the people you work with.

- Seek advice and say specifically why you came to that person.
- Create opportunities for people to be physically in the same place (like shared breaks) and reasons to connect with others in that shared space.
- Greet people in the morning.
- Tell someone at work you care and why.
- Show someone you care by doing something kind.
- Learn about the people you lead and talk to them about what matters to them.
- Laugh with someone.

Relationship-Based Workplaces

As an educator, you know trust and belonging in a classroom create a place where students feel safe enough to be creative and try new things. Educators spend a lot of time building a classroom climate and relationships throughout the school year. These relationship-based classrooms are students' most successful learning spaces (Poulou, 2017, 2018). But what about the workplace?

One of the largest studies about how this plays out in the workplace comes from Google's Project Aristotle (as cited in Duhigg, 2016). This project set out to answer one big question: What makes the best, highest-performing team? Project researchers looked at over 180 teams and gathered thousands of pieces of data. They considered things like IQ, personality measures, and levels of education. Not one of these individual measures made any difference to the teams' performance level. There was no profile of the perfect performer, so who was on the teams was unimportant. Only the following two things predicted high performance (Achor, 2018; Duhigg, 2016).

1. People on the team understood the power of social connection with one another.
2. People had an environment where they felt safe to take risks and be vulnerable with one another.

People on teams displaying these qualities knew it was OK to make mistakes. People on these teams also knew the other members had their back and wouldn't reject or punish them for speaking up. In other words, these people were safe and felt like they belonged—exactly like students in successful classrooms.

In his book *Big Potential*, author, speaker, and positive psychology advocate Shawn Achor (2018) talks about Google's study, as well as his own study of Harvard students, in which he set out to find individual student attributes that would predict their level of happiness and success. He gathered all kinds of data from students, including grade point averages, entrance exam scores, hours of sleep, family income, and so on, and yet he found absolutely no connection between these individual measures and happiness or success (Achor, 2018). Like Google's study, Achor (2018) finds that *social connection* is the one great predictor of thriving both personally and academically. Social connection is also the best predictor of emotional well-being and optimism.

When you think about that, it makes sense. If I asked you to tell me about your best day at work, what would you tell me? I predict your story is not about the time you read a whole lot of report cards or finished a budget. I suspect your story would be about how excited the students were about a project they were working on together. You would tell me about how engaged they were in learning, especially the students whose eyes just lit up with pride when they showed you what they had done. Or maybe you would tell me about a project you worked on with your team. It could even have been about a report or budget, but whatever the project was, the story is likely about how much you laughed and how you and your team came up with some crazy ideas together. I imagine you might pause at this point in your story and tell me some of those ideas were actually surprisingly valuable. You, of course, would be smiling and chuckling a bit by this point as you recalled the memory, and I would be smiling along with you as our serotonin and oxytocin surged.

If you asked me about my best day at work, all my stories would be about times when I felt safe, connected, and inspired. I would tell you about the meetings when my team was *in the zone* of exchanging creative ideas. My team included friends and trusted colleagues, and I didn't even have to think about social safety because it was already there; it was a given. When you don't have to worry about social safety or status, you are free to be creative and move your collective work to the next level. These types of teams are more productive and do better work, and as an additional bonus, the people on them are happier and healthier (Achor, 2018).

The benefit of a caring team is that oxytocin lowers members' level of *cortisol*, a stress hormone. That, in turn, boosts members' immune system and makes them healthier (Kasos et al., 2018). In fact, social connection is comparable with quitting smoking as a predictor of life expectancy and exceeds many well-known risk factors for mortality, like levels of obesity or inactivity (Holt-Lunstad, Smith, & Layton, 2010).

That is powerful stuff! If you are a leader—and particularly if you are a human resource professional or are responsible for staffing in any way—then you know the financial and personal benefits of having a healthy workforce. Healthy staff come to work and work harder and better. Since both stress and other feelings (good and bad) are contagious, then you can see the effect belonging can have in a workplace. Beyond these economic benefits, if leaders can support people to live longer and healthier lives, those leaders will be doing important ethical work that benefits everyone.

Belonging Cues and Action Strategies

So how do education leaders take advantage of all these amazing benefits of social connection? How do leaders create cultures of belonging in their schools, homes, and workplaces? You can find one answer in best-selling author Daniel Coyle's (2018) book *The Culture Code*. Coyle (2018) looks inside some of the world's most successful organizations and finds the most important thing high-performing teams share is high levels of what he calls *belonging cues*. Belonging cues are behaviors like proximity, eye contact, attention, and turn taking. These behaviors create safe connections in groups. Belonging cues have the following three basic qualities.

1. **Energy:** People are invested in the exchange in some way, such as the following.
    - Show up and show interest.
    - Make gentle eye contact. (There are cultural differences related to eye contact, so be aware of cultural norms and don't hold eye contact for too long or expect it back in the same way.)
    - Smile.
    - Ask open-ended questions.
    - Expect input from everyone.
    - Overcommunicate that you are listening.
    - Avoid interrupting.
    - Model and expect risk taking.
    - Create time and space for social connection before, after, or during meetings.

2. **Individualization:** People are treated as unique and valued, as the following exemplify.
   - Be explicit about why each person's and the collective's skills are important to the work.
   - Ask for help and explain why you asked a particular person or group.
   - Connect people when you notice complementary skill sets or interests.
   - Give and expect clear, direct feedback.
   - Embrace the messenger.
   - Know and ask about people's lives.
   - Create space for everyone to have a voice and expect them to contribute.
   - Step back and let your team do the work.
   - Use feelings as data.
3. **Future orientation:** People receive signals that the relationship will continue, such as the following.
   - Encourage people to speak up about problems, and coach them through problem-solving processes.
   - Prepare and practice for new practices or activities.
   - Embed reflection and improvement as continuous practices.
   - Connect the work you are doing with the people you are doing it for. For example, if you are working on improving mathematics learning and teaching practices, start by imagining what the end results will look like—engaged students playing and learning mathematics concepts together and having success.
   - Have a code word or phrase that indicates the need to go back and clarify something before moving on.
   - Be a connector beyond the current project you are working on.
   - Signpost future relationships by saying things like, "The next time we work together," "I am always so excited when we get to work together," or even something as simple as, "See you soon!" Such statements all signpost the pact that your relationship will continue even if the project or position does not.
   - Highlight relationships at times of transition, like onboarding, new roles, and staff transitions or retirements.

One phrase can sum up the actions inherent in each of these belonging cues: *you are safe*. When you use belonging cues, you show the other person the interaction is important, you uniquely value the person's contributions, and your relationship with the person will continue beyond this job or project.

It is also important to know it is not enough to use these belonging cues just once; to be effective, you must repeatedly use belonging cues (Coyle, 2018). This makes sense from an evolutionary perspective, as the brain is designed to defend against danger and sees a lack of connection to the group as certain death. When you experience belonging cues, your brain settles into safety and frees you to focus on the task in front of you from a place of security and connection.

The degree to which people feel safe and connected matters more for performance than what information they have, the format of the meeting, the facilitation of that meeting, and so on (Coyle, 2018; Van Swol & Kane, 2018).

Belonging cues are powerful in the workplace. Coyle (2018) writes about a *sociometer* that measures belonging cues in conversation. He finds in study after study, in different types of workplaces and projects, it is possible to predict performance by ignoring all the informational context in the exchanges and focusing only on belonging cues. Just think about the implications of this. The degree to which people feel safe and connected matters more for performance than what information they have, the format of the meeting, the facilitation of that meeting, and so on (Coyle, 2018; Van Swol & Kane, 2018). So how do leaders harness the power of belonging cues and the brain's biological desire for connection to create happier, healthier, and more productive teams? How do leaders put this research into action and practice?

Leaders can create belonging and support connection in three ways.

1. Lead with relationships.
2. Make connections explicit.
3. Promote flourishing by connecting to passion.

Because belonging only happens in relationships, I begin there.

Lead With Relationships

You should have a relationship with everyone who directly reports to you. There is a bit of debate about the number of people you can have meaningful connections with, especially with increasing social media use (Wellman, 2012). British anthropologist and evolutionary psychologist Robin Ian MacDonald Dunbar's (1993) seminal research suggests the number of face-to-face interactions people can carry on in their social network at a time is limited to around 150 people. This is commonly referred to as *Dunbar's number*. However, more recent research suggests people's ability to maintain connection is far more complex than a single number (Lindenfors, Wartel, & Lind, 2021). In any case, I suspect the actual number is less important than the idea that if you can't remember someone's name and at least one or two things about the person, then it is time to either get to know the person or find some way to share the leadership responsibility with someone else who will.

The important part is not for you to be friends with everyone on your teams, but to have some *connection* with all team members and care about them. Getting to know a little bit about someone will help with the connection and hopefully the care, but if you notice you are struggling with the care part, you may have to dig in a little more. You may need to address a behavior in the person, in yourself, or in your relationship that is interfering.

Check yourself to see what it is about this person that is triggering something in you. Some of the self-awareness practices from chapter 2 (page 23) will come in handy here, so remember to start there to make sure you are approaching your relationships with clear intention and ownership of your own position. Everyone arrives in a relationship with previous experiences and assumptions, so it is important to be aware of them.

For example, I have heard a few times about young teachers not wanting to work full time. Some I have encountered use the term *yoga Fridays* to describe this situation. This term is a convenient way to comment on these young teachers' commitment (or lack thereof) and refers to the belief that these teachers are lazy and want life easy in a way different from the struggle and hard work of more experienced teachers.

If you are a leader with this impression of young teachers, then you are arriving with assumptions and judgments about people even before your relationships begin. Self-awareness allows you to notice and challenge assumptions potentially damaging to relationships. It is your job as a leader to start with yourself. As you will remember from chapter 2, self-awareness is a practice, so perfection is not the goal.

After you look at your own reactions and assumptions, then encouraging others to do the same is also a good idea. Providing time and space for everyone to reflect on what they value, what they are passionate about, and how they show up at work can have a powerful impact on individuals and promote understanding and connection within teams (Boell & Senge, 2016).

Canadian province education ministries support many leaders to study and practice *compassionate systems leadership*, a systems-change framework the Center for

Systems Awareness inspired (https://systemsawareness.org). The practice of checking in at the beginning of meetings allows each person to notice what is going on. This short amount of time lets people check in with their feelings, thoughts, and intentions, and can help individuals arrive to meetings with self-awareness. When there is an opportunity to share check-in information with others, people get different perspectives and some empathy for the others in their group, and they start to build connections with one another. (See page 67 for the reproducible, "Check-In Protocol for Building Self-Awareness, Team Connection, and Belonging.") Another check-in option is to have staff join you in a short meditation or focus exercise (see figure 3.1).

> We are just going to take a moment to check in with ourselves before we start today. You can do this sitting or standing, so I invite you to either sit or stand—whatever is most comfortable for you. I invite you to close your eyes or lower your gaze if that works better for you. Take a moment to check in with yourself. It is sometimes helpful to take a few long, slow, deep breaths in and out through your nose to begin this process, as this helps to slow and calm the nervous system.
>
> As you breathe in and out slowly, you may want to put your hands on your belly and notice how it fills up with air when you breathe in and how it deflates like a balloon as you take that long, deep breath out. Take a moment to just notice the process of your breath and focus on the breath moving in and out of your belly. If thoughts come into your mind, just notice them without judgment, and then focus back on breathing. (Wait through a couple of breaths here.)
>
> Now I invite you to check in for a moment with what is going on inside you. What do you notice in your body? Are there places in your body where you are feeling tension, pain, or discomfort? Just notice, and then try to breathe *into those areas* and see if you can release some of that tension by relaxing the muscles there. (Pause here.) Maybe parts of your body are feeling relaxed at the moment, and if they are, notice those areas too. Take a moment to scan your whole body. Notice the points of connection where your body meets the chair or your feet touch the floor; maybe move your fingers a little bit or wiggle your toes inside your shoes.
>
> As a way of ending our short reflection, I invite you to take one last long, deep breath in through your nose and out through your nose. Then, when you are ready, open your eyes and come back to the room.

Figure 3.1: Meditation script example.

*Visit **go.SolutionTree.com/educatorwellness** for a free reproducible version of this figure.*

Make Connections Explicit

Connections happen naturally because people are wired for them, but these connections happen better, faster, and stronger when leaders pay attention to and value these natural tendencies. In the classroom, educators know it matters if they greet students and connect with them when they arrive in the morning (Shields-Lysiak, Boyd, Iorio, & Vasquez, 2020). The same is true for adults. Adults like it when people acknowledge them and when others are happy to see them, so make it an intentional practice to greet the adults in your school when they arrive in the morning. Create space and opportunity for this to happen among your work team members.

This is not about the principal or the superintendent standing at the door to the school or office, cheering and high-fiving everyone as they walk through the front door. This is about encouraging and supporting intentional, authentic connections and relationships.

For staff members who work together in the school, having at least one good friend has significant protective factors for well-being (Mann, 2018). Staff members don't all have to be friends, but having friends at work is beneficial. It is not your job as the leader to organize friendships, but if you create space for them to happen naturally, they will. Do you have comfortable spaces where people will naturally gather? This is often a staff room or lunchroom in a district office, but it can also be a beautiful outside space to sit or walk. Is there time for checking in and connecting at the beginning of meetings?

If you are meeting others in person, think about encouraging a gathering time before the meeting in a device-free zone. Start your online meetings with a virtual check-in with small groups. One-to-one walking meetings are a great way to create and support connections, and these meetings have the bonus of movement and connection to nature if outside.

Promote Flourishing by Connecting to Passion

Leaders should also support and encourage things that inspire and energize educators. My friend and mentor, Sabre Cherkowski, and her co-researcher, Keith Walker (2016, 2018) have done a lot of research and work in this area. They talk about the power of noticing and nurturing things that make educators well and inspire their work (Cherkowski & Walker, 2018). (See page 68 for a reproducible, "Protocol for Appreciative Inquiry.")

The ability to reflect and energize starts with a bit of self- (and then group) reflection. As an example, I was part of a book club reading of *Designing Your*

Life: How to Build a Well-Lived, Joyful Life (Burnett & Evans, 2016) in which members did a noticing exercise. As book club members, we were tasked with noticing which activities during our workday gave us energy and enjoyment and which activities left us drained of energy and enthusiasm. We collected data over the course of a week or two. The idea is that if you notice which activities give you joy and energy, then you do more of those things. If you also find things that decrease your energy and enthusiasm, you do less of these activities or find a way to do them differently.

"Connecting with other principals working on the same things has been huge for me. It has helped cut down on so much time. . . . Why reinvent the wheel on parent letters, emails, reports, and other managerial tasks? I think it may have made these tasks slightly more enjoyable, but it has certainly freed up time, which definitely leads to more time for enjoyment!"

—Elementary principal (personal communication, August 2021)

You may be unable to avoid doing that report you don't want to do, but maybe you can find a way to do it in a more enjoyable way. For example, try doing the report with a colleague who is doing the same thing or while listening to music. Try sandwiching this task between two really great things you love to do. If you perform tasks with a group, then you get to see commonalities where you can grow and ways you can harness the other members' different skills and interests to increase the power and capacity of the work you do. Why do something you are unskilled at or not passionate about if you have a team member with those skills and interests? This is part of the power of the collective. When people connect with their own gifts and interests and can share these gifts with others, they increase their own enjoyment (which is contagious)—and they also increase their value to the group. It becomes a continuous loop of those feel-good hormones and belonging cues, which is a recipe for flourishing!

A Culture of Connection, Not Competition

The best teams work together for a common purpose. All team members know and own that purpose, and they support one another to get there together. It is important to watch for and question practices and systems that work on the carrot-and-stick model (the "carrot" being a reward and the "stick," a negative consequence) and focus on individual achievement over the achievements of the group. Belonging cues remind members they need to uniquely value each person, and that value should be in what each person brings to the group.

How can team members make a unique contribution to the collective goal or purpose, and how can you as a leader encourage and support them? Here are some ways to do that.

- **Get rid of all but the absolutely essential hierarchy:** The value of each employee should be based on how they are contributing to the overall goal of the organization and the teams they are a member of, not at what level of the hierarchy their position lands. Create a culture where communication is open up and down the positional hierarchy. Leaders cannot divide the message of belonging and connection by role because it is about the interconnectedness between people.

    Relationships know no hierarchy. If you treat your boss differently than you treat someone who reports to you, what message does that send? If you value the opinion of someone higher up in the hierarchy simply because of the person's position over the thoughts of someone who has more knowledge and experience but is lower in the hierarchy, what does that say about the value of people?

- **Question assumptions and disrupt narratives of traditional systems that historically advantaged some people and wisdom over others:** Whose voices are included in planning and decision making? It is important to have diverse voices contributing ideas and asking thoughtful questions. If everyone thought the same way, there would be no growth or change to move people forward. So look around the table and see who is sitting with you and sharing their voices. If you are trying to make a decision and consulting only people who have the same opinions as you or come from only similar cultures and life experiences, you are missing valuable wisdom. These are your opportunities for belonging and connection, but also for the best, most creative ideas.

    Be especially careful when you hear *othering* of any kind (for example, "the teachers," "the administration," "the district") as it is a huge anti-belonging cue. I remember being at a meeting with school staff, and people were upset about a decision. Suddenly, some staff began referring to the principal as "the administrator" instead of by name. *Othering* is the beginning of depersonalization, and it should raise huge alarm bells whenever you hear it. It is important for educators to have clear roles, and a system hierarchy is necessary structurally, but be thoughtful and reflective about when roles and the hierarchy are necessary and when they are getting in the way of relationships and creative, connected work.

- **Value Indigenous voices:** Although I can't do it justice in this book for many reasons, I would be negligent if I didn't include the value of Indigenous voice and knowledge, but these are particularly important in a chapter about belonging and connection. Indigenous cultures are inherently relational, and they have much to teach about the power of belonging. If you are working on well-being, listening to and including those with Indigenous knowledge are immensely powerful, and you should consider their inclusion essential.

- **Share problems with a larger group:** Do you have a problem you would like to solve? Why not throw it out there for *everyone* to solve? Put it on the staff room table to get ideas or toss it into the next group meeting to see if anyone can help. There is power in group creativity, and it may surprise you what people come up with.

"Sometimes, I listen to professional development about the importance of social connection and belonging, and I am so surprised that people have to learn this in a workshop. It is just what we have always known. It is embedded in what life is."

—Aboriginal support worker (personal communication, October 2021)

Leaders must enable these brave conversations about relationships not only because the relationships matter but also because people's brains are so wired for connection (and so on guard for the danger of disconnection), they can jump to inaccurate conclusions. These inaccurate stories can interfere with relationships and the great work people do together. If aware of this natural human tendency, leaders can prepare for it and work on preventing or disrupting it when it inevitably happens to themselves and others. (See "The Ladder of Inference," page 34.)

NEGATIVITY BIAS AND INACCURATE STORIES

People's brains are designed to protect, but they are imperfect, and sometimes they can get in the way. The first way this occurs is through something called *negativity bias*. A *negativity bias* is the brain's tendency to scan for negatives and focus on those bits of information over the positive or neutral (Hanson, 2018). Back in evolutionary history, it made sense for people to look for danger first as a way to protect themselves from predators and stay alive, so their brains were designed to scan the environment for danger first. People have a basic, biological tendency to register negative things first and interpret things from that negative perspective as well. Rick Hanson (2018), a psychologist and best-selling author, describes the brain's negativity bias as being like "Velcro for bad and Teflon for good" (p. 43), which is a powerful visual of this tendency.

Completing the story to reward is the other way people's brains have evolved. When something happens, people's brains are designed to make sense of it. People take in information, put together a story to explain the situation, and then their brains reward them for completing that story, whether accurate or not. Often, because of negativity bias, these stories are inaccurate, which can lead to misunderstandings and get in the way of the belonging and connection all people need.

A classic example of this is when I look over at my boss in a meeting and she looks serious. I am convinced what I just said has upset her, and she wants me off the project. That could all be true, of course, but as you have no doubt figured out, the odds of that are pretty slim. My brain chemistry doesn't care whether my story is accurate; instead, it rewards me with a hit of dopamine for *completing the story*. However, if I leave it at that, what does that do to our relationship? If I go to my boss and clarify things with her, more than likely, she will tell me she was thinking about what to make for dinner or was seriously considering my particularly relevant point, and all is well. Of course, if she actually is upset, that is also good for me to know so we can sort it out. Addressing the issue upsetting her stops the problem from spiraling into something bigger and possibly damaging our relationship.

It seems so simple, but until leaders know about the brain's negativity bias and consciously remember to recognize it, what often happens is they let these things go. So have a conversation about negativity bias with your teams. Use a code word or phrase for people to check out things with one another. For example, you may say, "I am having a lot of alarm bells going off right now, and this is leading me to think you are upset about what went on earlier in the meeting. I just wanted to check in with you. Were you upset earlier? Are we OK?" Brené Brown (2018), research professor, lecturer, author, and podcast host, calls this strategy "the story I am making up" (p. 247), and Coyle (2018) refers to it as *pulling the alarm code*. It doesn't matter what you call it, if you can recognize negativity bias and check how things are with others, you will avoid a lot of false assumptions and miscommunication.

Coyle (2018) also notes if people can settle that alarm with more accurate information, then their amazing brains start energetically searching for belonging signals from those now part of their team. For leaders, this is powerful information. It is important for you to recognize when someone triggers your negativity bias so you can check, maintain, or create relationships with the added bonus of modeling for others how to check out these assumptions. As a result, others on your team will feel more comfortable trying the strategy as well.

It is also important for leaders to know that if someone comes to you to check on something, you can fix the communication or other problem (if you are upset) or let them know there isn't anything to fix. Either way, this is the perfect time to shower the person with belonging cues because in that moment, the person's brain is highly receptive and open to a strengthened relationship. Going back to the other example, if my boss says, "Thanks for checking, but I was really just thinking about what you said," or "Thank you for bringing up that point; I really value the perspective you bring to the group because it opens up and challenges my thinking," not only does this new information lower my worries and stop the alarm bells but it also reinforces my connection to the team and the relationship I have with my boss. I feel both valued and cared about.

Review the scenarios in figure 3.2, and then use the reproducible, "Identifying Negativity Bias and Determining Actions and Belonging Cues" (page 70), to fill in possible negativity biases, actions, and belonging cues.

The Bottom Line

Being aware of negativity bias and explicitly discussing and preparing for it with your team are great ways to avoid this particular pitfall turning into a much larger problem. Being explicit and clear about communication in general promotes connection and group cohesion because at the base of connection and belonging is always safety. To be your best, most productive self, you must work in a place where you feel safe. For people to work together on the most productive and creative teams, members must establish and hold sacred safe spaces for one another.

Situation	Negativity Bias	Action	Belonging Cues
Gail looks over at her boss, Helena, during a meeting. Helena looks serious.	Gail is convinced what she just said has upset Helena, and now she is upset with Gail and wants her off the project.	After the meeting is over, Gail approaches Helena and says, "I saw you looked pretty serious while I was talking. Did I say something to upset you?" Helena responds, "Thanks for checking, but I was really just thinking about what you said. Thank you for bringing up that point. I really value the perspective you bring to the group because it really opens up and challenges my thinking. I was actually thinking hard about your idea of creating a community garden outside where people could socialize. Derrick might be a great collaborator; he's a gifted gardener. Apologies if I looked annoyed. I felt quite the opposite."	**Energy:** Gail made gentle eye contact with Helena and smiled while they spoke. **Individualization:** Helena suggested connecting Derrick and Gail when she noticed complementary interests. **Future Orientation:** Helena signposted future relationships.
Casey's face is red, and she is quieter than usual in a team planning meeting for an upcoming conference.	Marc, who is leading the meeting, thinks it looks like Casey was crying before the meeting. She is probably upset because she is not getting her way. She is always so emotional, and it is getting in the way of the work.	Marc is tempted to let it go because he is busy and doesn't want to encourage what he sees as unnecessary drama, but he also cares about Casey, so he waits until after the meeting and then asks, "I noticed you were a bit quiet in the meeting, Casey. Is everything OK?" "Yes," she says. "I was just noticing I talk a lot in meetings, and I was trying to do more listening. I guess I was right if you noticed the difference. Thanks for checking. Oh, and by the way, I know my face is a bit red this morning, but I went for a long walk before this meeting and you know what the wind does to my face!"	**Energy:** Marc's question after the meeting shows he is invested in the relationship and the planning project. **Individualization:** Marc noticed and asked about Casey, which signals he cares about her. **Future Orientation:** This moment of caring shows their relationship matters beyond the details of the planning meeting.

Figure 3.2: Examples of how identifying negativity bias and determining possible actions and belonging cues help leaders respond to situations.

Belonging and Connection Action Steps

1. Develop and encourage social connections at work. For example, encourage and support things like walking or exercise groups, book clubs, or any social activities people are interested in starting, or start one yourself to share your favorite activity.

2. Try a tech-free meeting with time before to gather and connect (always an invitation, not a requirement), and see what people think.

3. Use belonging cues over and over again. For example, "The work we are doing together matters," "You are unique and valued," and "This relationship will continue."

4. Create opportunities and physical spaces that foster connection. For example, make the staff room an inviting place with different areas that promote conversation or create an outside gathering space for staff.

5. Open up opportunities for creative ideas and problem solving across roles and up and down traditional hierarchies. For example, connect people across departments or in different roles who have similar interests or are working on similar or complementary matters.

6. Be aware of negativity bias and create a process to check out assumptions. For example, "Some strange alarm bells are going off for me. Can we circle back on some things and check them out? I am worried my suggestion may have stopped the previous conversation instead of adding to it, and I want to make sure I didn't cut off Vold's idea. Anything we missed, Vold?"

7. Notice and acknowledge how people contribute their unique talents to the group. For example, "I wanted to mention how much easier my work is after Colin showed us that tech tip the other day. It has made everyone's workflow much easier. I love that you share your knowledge with the team, Colin. Thank you."

8. Connect and share common administrative tasks to lighten everyone's load.

Check-In Protocol for Building Self-Awareness, Team Connection, and Belonging

Total time: Ten to fifteen minutes

Tools needed: A journal and a pen for each participant

Use the following steps to complete the check-in protocol.

1. Ask everyone to take a few minutes to reflect on a guiding question. You can do this by providing participants with a question or two to respond to, or by leading them through a short, guided meditation to encourage reflection (see figure 3.1, page 58).

   Possible guiding questions include the following.

   - What do you notice in your body right now? Are you feeling relaxed, tense, or tired? Notice where in your body you register this feeling.
   - How are you feeling today? What is going on for you right now, in this moment? How is your body feeling, and what thoughts are running through your head? Try for right now just to notice the feelings without judgment.
   - How are you arriving? Check in with yourself, and notice what is happening to you. Start with what is happening in your body. Notice if you feel tension anywhere or if there is a place where you feel calm. Without judgment, notice if there is anything from before you arrived that you are bringing into this meeting you could put down for a while. What do you need?

2. Take five minutes for everyone to individually journal about their reflection.

3. Move into groups of three to five and ask participants to share their personal reflections. Remind participants to only share what they are comfortable sharing and to take turns speaking. The amount of time can vary depending on your schedule, but even one to two minutes per person is enough. Remind everyone that the job of the listeners is to listen and hold space for the speaker without judgment or interpretation.

4. After the check-in exercise, thank everyone for holding space for one another. Check in with the whole group from time to time about how they are finding the exercise, but especially the first few times as you practice. This doesn't need to happen immediately, though it may make sense at the end of the meeting as a checkout.

Protocol for Appreciative Inquiry

Who am I at my best?

Think back to a time in any aspect of your life when you felt you were living the "real you" with a feeling of *excitement and energy*, a time when you wanted to find new ways to keep doing the things that made you feel *alive*, *engaged*, and *inspired*.

What were you doing, and why were you doing these things?	Who were you with, or who helped you to engage in these ways?	What did you feel as you engaged in these activities and ways of being?

Bring your full awareness and all your senses to your reflection.

What did you see, feel, hear, or even taste?

What were your facial expressions during these moments?

> As you recall your narrative, think back to a time in your work (or target area of life) when you felt these experiences. Describe in detail what was going on (both inside and outside your body).

page 1 of 2

Beyond Self-Care © 2023 Solution Tree Press • SolutionTree.com
Visit **go.SolutionTree.com/educatorwellness** to download this free reproducible.

In our school, we _____.

Now imagine you had a magic wand and could create whatever you wanted or needed to develop an environment that would foster and support this greatest version of you in your work role.

 What would you create?

What would it look like for you to live that expression of who you are when you are at your best?	What is one small thing you could do right now to live that expression of who you are?	With whom will you share this appreciative inquiry?

As you think about this appreciative inquiry experience, what other stories of past experiences or dreams of the future are you inspired to share?

Who else might you share this experience with so that you might work together to build a community to support and help one another grow toward flourishing?

Source: Cherkowski, S., & Walker, K. (2018). Teacher wellbeing: Noticing, nurturing, sustaining, and flourishing in schools. Burlington, Ontario, Canada: Word & Deed.

Identifying Negativity Bias and Determining Actions and Belonging Cues

Situation	Negativity Bias	Action	Belonging Cues
			Energy: People are invested in the exchange in some way. **Individualization:** People are treated as unique and valued. **Future Orientation:** People give signals that the relationship will continue.
			Energy: People are invested in the exchange in some way. **Individualization:** People are treated as unique and valued. **Future Orientation:** People give signals that the relationship will continue.
			Energy: People are invested in the exchange in some way. **Individualization:** People are treated as unique and valued. **Future Orientation:** People give signals that the relationship will continue.

Beyond Self-Care © 2023 Solution Tree Press • SolutionTree.com
Visit **go.SolutionTree.com/educatorwellness** to download this free reproducible.

The *Other* Psychological Safety

Psychological safety isn't about being nice. It's about giving candid feedback, openly admitting mistakes, and learning from each other.
—Amy C. Edmondson

The single best way to promote a sense of belonging and all of the great outcomes of having a connected team is to create a sense of psychological safety in the work environment. You may be tempted to skip this chapter because, as a school or district leader, you may be fairly certain that although not everyone on your team is always perfectly happy, they are definitely safe. Your assumption may be right. Still—don't skip this chapter. There's more to learn.

I have worked in many schools and departments where the culture is safe and staff are encouraged to try new things and learn from those lessons or projects that don't quite go the way they had planned. If you have had the good fortune to work in one of these places, you know that feeling.

I have been on many such teams, and just thinking about the people on them and the work we got to do together makes me smile as I write this. These are not wildly utopian places where everything is perfect, they are places where people can use their energy for work rather than using it up in unproductive conflict or self-protection. You can feel the energy in a workplace like that. These are places that, when you visit, you often wish you could stay for a while, get to know people a little more, and be part of what they are creating together. When you work in a place like this, you can bring your whole self to work. Your colleagues know something about you and can support and challenge you. When you know others care about you and your team values you, it frees up your energy for creative work.

This chapter begins by presenting the qualities and effects of a psychologically safe workplace and contrasting these with psychologically unsafe spaces. It then discusses two ways leaders can help build a psychologically safe workplace: (1) through positive leader relations and (2) through workplace supports and work design. I'll then contemplate the importance of leader fallibility before finishing with a series of helpful action steps.

A Psychologically Safe Workplace

I don't want to oversimplify a complex system, but psychological safety becomes cyclical. In a place where you feel safe, you are open to receiving and sharing ideas, which leads to more creative work and more connection (Greenbaum, Bonner, Mawritz, Butts, & Smith, 2020). The more connected you feel, the more you want to contribute, which makes you feel valued, and the cycle continues (see figure 4.1).

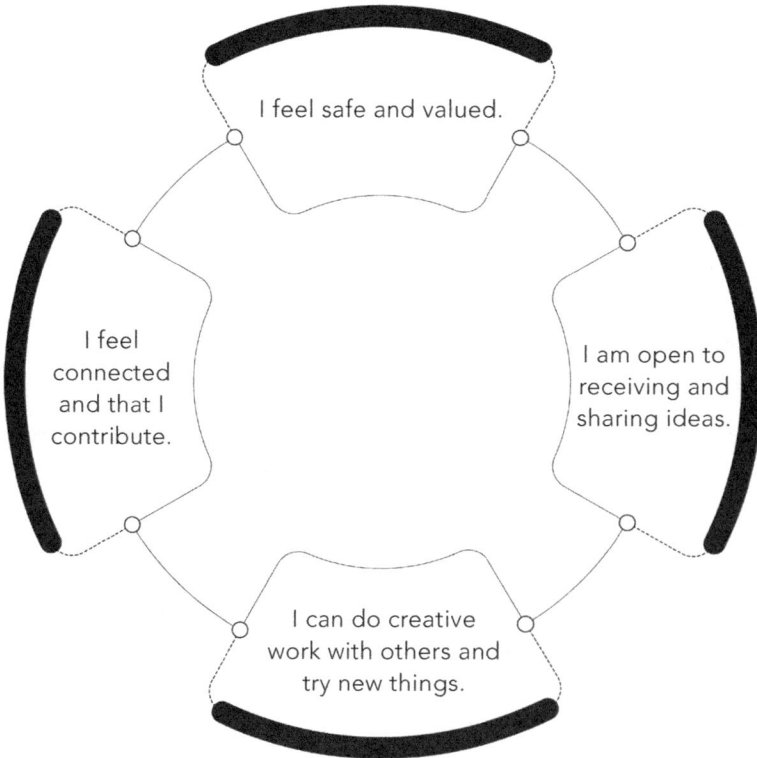

Figure 4.1: The cycle of safety.

Sinek (2014) writes about a similar circle he calls the *circle of safety* and tells leaders it is their job to create circles where people care about one another, so teams do their best work.

"It was one of the best workplaces I have ever worked in. We gathered every Friday and planned together. It was a unique group of people, but it worked somehow. We shared a lot of laughter and so many unique and unusual situations, but I always knew the team and the principal had my back 100 percent."

—Former alternate school teacher, personal communication, November 10, 2021

"As a leader, I made sure we stayed within a box, but it was a really big box, and inside that, we could be wildly creative."

—Principal at the same school, personal communication, November 10, 2021

What happens if you would like to work this way but you have been assigned to a school or work team that does not run with psychological safety in mind? School communities are complex systems full of people with different stories and experiences they bring to work. Along with the individuals' own experiences, the community itself comes with an identity—a story—that shapes what happens there. So, what happens when you arrive in a school or workplace with a difficult or closed culture, or something happens to create a situation where the workplace becomes unsafe? Figure 4.2 (page 74) shows the cycle that happens in psychologically unsafe workplaces.

What will you see in workplaces with low psychological safety? Sometimes you see the lack of psychological safety clearly, like a school my colleague visited where she heard a group of education assistants talking about an after-school meeting and their plan to intentionally arrive late. While I didn't know specific information about this group, imagine what experiences members must have had up to that point to have this mindset. It didn't come from nowhere, and it was clear they had developed some high walls to protect themselves, which is what happens when people feel powerless to confront a toxic environment.

Often the fear from a lack of psychological safety is much more underground or hidden, which can be even more damaging than outward displays. I want to

Figure 4.2: An unsafe cycle.

continue the story of Diane, who you met in chapter 3 (page 45). Diane worked on many excellent teams, but she also had one experience working in an unsafe work environment. The following story is a clear example of what can happen when things become unsafe and the impact that can have on the health, happiness, and success of individuals, their families, and their workplaces. In Diane's case, very few people around her had any awareness of what was happening. Remember the Sunday night test? This was the one time she definitely didn't pass that test. It was the only time she ever dreaded going to work.

> *Diane assumed that the changes she noticed in her boss, Elaina, were due to the increased pressure Elaina was experiencing. She noticed a withdrawal of communication, a lot of canceled meetings, and what felt like avoidance. Then Diane found out her position was being cut, which was quite a surprise to her. She was disappointed but wondered if that was the reason Elaina had been distant and stressed lately. It was a bit of a relief to finally make sense of what she was seeing. She was looking forward to meeting with Elaina to talk about it.*
>
> *However, it turns out Diane had the story wrong because when they met, Diane was both devastated and shocked when Elaina said she didn't want*

> anything to do with her anymore. Elaina said she would tolerate her presence and be polite, but the committees and projects they worked on together were Elaina's space and that Diane would have to think about what she wanted to do about that. It was a clear message that Diane wasn't welcome.
>
> At that meeting, Elaina gave no explanation as to what Diane had done to provoke her or what she should have done differently. Eventually, Elaina explained that over the course of the previous year, she had been hearing things from someone else that led her to believe Diane was saying negative things about Elaina and the decisions she and the district made. Diane and Elaina had worked together successfully for years. They had enjoyed an excellent working relationship and cared about each other, but now that trust and respect had been destroyed over something Diane never did.
>
> Diane thought, "I would never say anything negative about Elaina because, first of all, I didn't think anything negative about her. If I did have a problem with something she was doing, I still wouldn't say things behind her back. I would go to her directly and ask what was going on. Why didn't she do that for me?"

Research proves that psychological safety is "positively related to employee engagement, task performance, satisfaction, and commitment" (Frazier, Fainshmidt, Klinger, Pezeshkan, & Vracheva, 2017, p. 140). During that time, Diane was a perfect example of someone struggling with all of those things. It was difficult for her to get anything done, as she became obsessed with understanding and fixing the situation with Elaina. This situation is a perfect example of how feeling, thinking, and acting work together, so the stress impacted Diane on all three levels.

I suspect if I could talk to the other people involved in this story, I would see they were also feeling unsafe and struggling with similar feelings. Let's look at the impact this work environment had on Diane.

> Diane felt terrible, full of fear and worry about everything she said or did. She would sit in meetings and feel her heart race. She would check her heart rate, and it would be wild, even though she was just sitting in a meeting. She eventually went to the doctor and had them run a stress test just to make sure that the pain in her chest really was just stress and not some kind of medical condition.
>
> Diane was so distracted she had little energy to focus on tasks at work. She spoke up less and tried to stay out of the way at work. There was a time when there were only certain hallways in the building she would walk down.
>
> At home, her family struggled to support her. She had trouble focusing on what was happening in her family's world because she was so obsessed with

> *fixing what was happening at work. Diane dove into books and podcasts to feed her brain and did all the self-care practices she could to heal her body and spirit.*

Diane was now part of the underground, making it more difficult to recognize the unsafe workplace because she didn't talk to anyone at work about what was going on. First, it was embarrassing, but Elaina was also a highly respected leader in the school district, so she wondered what would happen if she spoke up and whether doing so would be helpful for anyone. Even more important for Diane was she still really cared about Elaina and knew she was a good person and an excellent leader who had just made a mistake. Diane still hoped they could repair the relationship someday, even though it would be difficult.

This kind of unsafe culture is more difficult to recognize unless you are looking for it, and it is much more difficult to address. The other factor that complicates things further, particularly if you are a senior leader, is even though you may be well connected with your team and quite sure you would know if there is a culture or safety problem in your organization, chances are if there is one, no one would tell you. The culture of feedback, growth, and learning educators value so much for students in the classroom is sometimes missing in the education workplace, and when it does exist, it rarely moves up the hierarchy.

Psychological Safety, Defined

Psychological safety is a construct that has generated a great deal of research, which highlights the importance of creating a sense of safety in the workplace (Frazier et al., 2017). In their article *"Psychological Safety: The History, Renaissance, and Future of an Interpersonal Construct,"* coauthors Amy C. Edmondson and Zhike Lei (2014) note, "Feeling safe is what allows people to grow, learn, contribute, and perform effectively in a rapidly changing world" (p. 40). Although similar to other constructs, like feelings of empowerment and work engagement (which refer to how individuals each feel about themselves and their particular role), psychological safety is more about how individuals each perceive their general work environment (Frazier et al., 2017).

Psychological safety is similar but distinct from the concept of *trust*, which people are often more familiar with. If you trust someone on your team, you give the person the benefit of the doubt and believe the person will do what the person says and act with integrity. Psychological safety is when you believe others will give *you* the benefit of the doubt and not shame or punish you for speaking up (Edmondson, 2019).

In a psychologically safe workplace, people are more open to change, they generate ideas, and they admit to and learn from their mistakes. Although much of the psychological safety research comes from the business world, it is generalizable to all kinds of workplaces and organizations (Edmondson, 2019). In education, psychological safety is not a new concept; educators have promoted this way of interacting in classrooms, so it makes sense to think about how this type of environment is also important in the education workplace.

Return to the classroom again for a moment. Educators are clear about creating a classroom climate that allows and encourages students to take risks, try new ideas, and learn from their mistakes. They tell their students there are no stupid questions, and understand that clear feedback helps growth and learning. Where I live in Canada, the Province of British Columbia (n.d.) explains its vision for student success:

> To develop new models, the Ministry consulted with experts in the field. They suggested that to prepare students for the future, the curriculum must be learner-centred and flexible and maintain a focus on literacy and numeracy, while supporting deeper learning through concept-based and competency-driven approaches.
>
> The redesign of curriculum maintains a focus on sound foundations of literacy and numeracy while supporting the development of citizens who are competent thinkers and communicators, and who are personally and socially competent in all areas of their lives. British Columbia's redesigned curriculum honours the ways in which students think, learn, and grow, and prepares them for a successful lifetime of learning where ongoing change is constant.

It is encouraging to see this focus for students, but leaders need to take these skills and this wisdom from the classrooms to *all levels of the organization.* In the education workplace, there is often tension between the traditional human resources practices, which focus on creating rules and applying those rules consistently for everyone (based on job category), and classroom practices, which encourage educators each to provide equitable supports and learning opportunities that value their gifts based on what students need. This inconsistency is particularly problematic for young educators, who have learned in their not-so-distant student experiences to speak up, ask questions, and contribute something of value to the group.

If you have had the privilege of listening to senior high school students present their graduate portfolio documenting their learning journey, accomplishments, and plans, you will see that educators are doing a fairly good job of supporting psychological safety for students. These portfolios encourage students to talk about their accomplishments and plans for the future, and they inform learning by inviting leaders in students' chosen fields to listen to students present so those students can ask questions and share ideas with these experts. I have had the privilege of being invited to listen to several of these graduation portfolio presentations and learned just as much from these students as they have from me. But what happens when some of these former students become your employees? Do they hear the same messages? Are they able to apply the same skills you have taught them and share their valuable gifts in the workplace?

Of course, these questions don't only apply to young educators. Many more experienced educators and school leaders often feel caught in a position where they receive direction and are told to pass on that direction with little ability or perceived ability to ask questions about rules and practices that may not make sense to them (Wang, Pollock, & Hauseman, 2021). Is a teacher or a school principal given the same latitude and encouragement as the students in classrooms to ask questions, be curious, and contribute their ideas to support collective goals? For example, sometimes, it is not the senior leaders who have the most information about a certain topic or practice. Do senior leaders invite people in different roles to share this wisdom or ask questions if they are curious about practices or decisions?

School leaders often find themselves in difficult positions where policies, practices, and directives may not fit their own values or what they believe to be in the best interest of their school communities (Wang, 2018). Leaders can get stuck in a place where they feel like they have to choose between the best interest of their communities and doing or saying what district, state or provincial, or even federal representatives tell them to do or say. When this happens, principals report different strategies they use to make things work. They do what makes sense to them, even if it means finding creative work-arounds or intentionally ignoring directives. Chapter 5 (page 95) explores the idea of *subversive leadership* further, but it is important to be aware: one of the dangers of work-arounds is the impact they can have on relationships and perceived trust, which are important considerations for safety in the workplace.

In a study of self-awareness, trust, and feedback in leadership, researchers and coauthors Ngaio Crook, Ozar N. Alakavuklar, and Ralph Bathurst (2021) note about society:

> We expect that adults are capable of making decisions, contributing ideas and knowledge, dealing with ambiguity, and navigating complex

problems, but such expectation is suspended as people enter the workplace and re-assign that responsibility to others all in the name of leadership. (pp. 359–360)

Crook and colleagues (2021) ask whether assigning this responsibility to leaders allows people to avoid the complexities and anxiety of group dynamics, and creates an unrealistic type of *heroic leadership*, which is not helpful to anyone. One of the grievances I often hear in my work with principals is their confusion about what to do when staff expect them to solve so many of their problems. A young vice-principal once told me it was like staff expected her to have all the answers just because of her new title. This romanticism of the leadership position is not good for the leader or the staff because it takes away responsibility and efficacy and limits the contributions and value each individual can share with the group (Collinson, Jones, & Grint, 2017). It also places an impossible burden on leaders who already experience high levels of work intensification and can't possibly take on what should be collective tasks (Wang et al., 2018). Leaders themselves struggle with this idea of heroic leadership as they are often aware of and want to move toward more collaborative, shared leadership models and different ways of working. However, leaders also acknowledge the leader-knows-all (and often does-all) view is still very much part of the traditional system of education (Crook et al., 2021).

So how do leaders create psychological safety in the education workplace? A meta-analysis of the research on psychological safety finds two particular areas where you can have an impact: (1) positive leader relations and (2) workplace supports and design (Frazier et al., 2017).

Positive Leader Relations

Although leaders don't need to be (nor should they be) heroes to their staff, the relationships leaders have with those they lead do have an important impact on psychological safety (Yang, Li, Liang, & Zhang, 2021). Establishing connections and relationships is key to people feeling safe in their workplaces. Start by questioning the need for the hierarchy and all the structures that divide educators instead of promoting the fact that everyone is working toward a common goal: student learning.

Of course, some organizational structure is necessary, and role clarity is particularly important, but leaders must question power structures, rules, and practices that may no longer support the present-day goals of education. Consider the following examples.

- If a school is to foster a safe and inclusive learning environment where all students and staff feel safe and have a sense of belonging, do the organization's practices reflect that? Whose voices are included in conversations and decision making?

- If a school is focused on teaching critical-thinking and communication skills, do leaders expect and encourage staff to also use and celebrate those skills in the workplace? Or do leaders and staff avoid difficult conversations or engage in counterproductive practices just because "that's the way they've always been done"?
- If a school aims to truly integrate Aboriginal perspectives and knowledge in classrooms, is it fair to ask whether those same practices and ways of being also integrate in school and district meetings?

Leaders report struggling with their desire to act more relationally and less hierarchically, but the traditional mental models, explanations of "how things work," and the traditional structure of many education systems constrain them (Crook et al., 2021). It's important to consider which practices connect and inspire staff to work together and which get in the way by valuing some voices over others. In her book *The Fearless Organization*, Edmondson (2019) writes about the importance of reframing the role of the boss. She claims the traditional view of the boss as the ultimate authority who makes the decisions, sets the direction, tells subordinates what to do, and then judges how well they have done it, is a setup for fear (Edmondson, 2019). This traditional way of seeing the relationship moves people quickly into the default response of self-protection.

I remember asking a now-retired principal what he thought about a particular change my school district was implementing. He told me it didn't matter what he thought as he was an agent of the board. His comment certainly stopped the conversation between two knowledgeable and capable people because if the school district didn't allow him to have an opinion, then I certainly wasn't safe or valuable enough to have one. I have often thought of his answer and wondered about the message it sent. Ultimately, the senior leaders are tasked with setting direction. But what if, instead of being the decision makers telling people what to do, leaders were the people who set direction for continued growth and created space and conditions for that continued growth through creative solutions? See figure 4.3 for considerations when creating conditions for growth and creative solutions.

There are some specific actions you can take to help support positive leader relationships. The following sections explore examples of actions you and the teams you lead can do together: (1) rebalance social power, (2) place value on care, collegiality, collaboration, and collective accountability, (3) use information power for good, and (4) beware of messaging.

With your team, consider the following.

- What problem are we solving? Make sure the problem is clear and everyone in the group is working to solve the same thing.
- Why do we need to solve this problem?
- What knowledge and skills do we need? Who has them?
- Who are we missing?
- What will it look like if we are successful?
- Are we the right people to solve this problem? (Ensure you communicate clear boundaries—for example, budget, timeline, and so on—or if you need to hand the problem over to a different group.)
- Do we need or want anyone else's wisdom and knowledge to help inform our decision?
- Are we listening or reading with a learner's mind?
- Are we asking clarifying questions?
- How will we communicate our decision and why we chose it?
- Have we thanked everyone for their ideas and contributions?
- Have we set a date to review how things are going?
- Do we need to revise any of our decisions?

Figure 4.3: Creating conditions for growth and creative solutions.

Rebalance Social Power

A study on educational psychological safety finds years of experience and higher positions in the hierarchy increased psychological safety among educators (Edmondson, Higgins, Singer, & Weiner, 2016). It is a reminder that the more social power you have in a group, the more safety you enjoy. This should encourage formal and informal leaders to cultivate an awareness of their own social position and reflect on and disrupt the status and power imbalances in their organizations. Sometimes rebalancing social power is as simple as noticing and being curious about some of the assumptions guiding your practices. For example, who forms your committees? Are all your district committees groups of administrators, or groups of people in different roles representing different perspectives? If your committee members represent different roles, is everyone's voice heard and valued? Rebalancing social power can also provide opportunities for more voices to be heard.

When senior teachers and administrators are aware of their increased power and safety, they should speak up or ask questions to encourage other voices. For example, a new teacher or education assistant may have an idea to contribute about a school event, but staff members who run this event every year always do things a certain way. What would happen if a staff member who had been at the school for a while asked the newcomer to talk about his or her idea, encouraging the education assistant to speak up?

Formal and informal leaders can use their awareness of their own social power to raise questions and encourage involvement and ideas from others. In a meeting, who is quiet? Ask these members what they think or encourage them to share something, particularly if you know they have a connection with the topic. Even better, get everyone to think about the topic or problem on their own and then share what they write. In an online meeting, use a *waterfall chat*, where everyone puts their thoughts in the chat and presses Send at the same time. Both writing down thoughts individually and using the waterfall chat reduce the likelihood of everyone moving toward the ideas of the person with the most power or the strongest voice before everyone has a chance to share their thoughts.

If you plan to call on someone directly, give the person a warning to prepare by saying something like, "In a minute, I am going to ask those who haven't had a chance to speak yet to share their thoughts so we don't miss anyone's ideas." As a formal or informal leader, you may also need to step back sometimes to create safe spaces for others to share their wisdom and to give yourself the opportunity for deep listening. If there is someone on your team who tends to contribute a lot and speaks more often than others, it would be a great practice for them to try as well. Deep listening, learning to ask thoughtful questions, or both are also good to practice if you need to develop these skills.

You may want to tell your team members you are doing this, particularly if it is a big change for you. One time while practicing giving others space and deep listening, staff interpreted my actions as me being upset because it was so unusual. It was a reminder to be clear about my intention—this was a practice I clearly needed to do more often. Deep listening is also a great way to create a sense of collective accountability, where people know I not only want their participation but also deem it necessary for the team to be successful.

The following are a few strategies for rebalancing social power and creating collective responsibility.

- Let people know you value and expect everyone's contribution.
- Notice when someone is quiet and ask the person's thoughts.

- Make a connection to the knowledge you know someone has so the person can share it with the group.
- Give everyone time for individual reflection before answering questions.
- Use a waterfall chat in online meetings, where everyone hits *Send* at the same time.
- Give a warning when you plan to call on someone directly.
- Step back sometimes for deep listening.
- Encourage frequent contributors to step back sometimes too.

Place Value on Care, Collegiality, Collaboration, and Collective Accountability

Positive leader relationships also must include shared accountability for the work. A study of principals' experiences with the move to remote learning during the COVID-19 pandemic is a reminder that positive relationships are more than just being nice to one another (Weiner, Francois, Stone-Johnson, & Childs, 2021). This study finds that schools with low psychological safety often get the caring part right (Weiner et al., 2021). During this challenging switch to remote learning, the principals in both high- and low-psychological safety schools checked in with teachers and offered empathy and opportunities for connection. The principals reported holding virtual happy hours or calling periodically to check in and see how individual staff members were doing.

In schools with high psychological safety, the principals put great value on both care and collegiality, but the main difference was the principals also focused on *collective accountability*. As Weiner and colleagues (2021) state, "Principals also recalled the ways teachers' collaboration toward enhancing practice intensified during the pandemic, especially as they witnessed teachers familiar with technology support less experienced colleagues" (p. 14). This collaborative support between teachers and administrators was the differentiating factor between high- and low-psychological safety cultures. In high-psychological safety cultures, teachers and principals took joint responsibility for supporting one another and determining how to support student learning in this new and constantly changing environment. Although this particular study was conducted during the COVID-19 pandemic, I suspect there was a pre-pandemic culture of safety and connection at each of these schools, which created the understanding and expectation for everyone to help one another. If a community of educators feels their leader supports and cares about them in regular times, these educators will naturally rally around one another in times of stress and crisis because it's their natural human tendency. If the educators don't feel safe and that their leader cares about them, then when their leader (or someone else) does show care during a crisis, the educators will tend to see this as inauthentic, even when it is not.

The principal of one of the low-psychological safety schools in this study called teachers to see how they were doing—and they wondered why he was calling (Weiner et al., 2021). He may have authentically cared about how they were doing, but the teachers perceived the calls as the principal checking up on them. In one of the high-psychological safety schools, the principal talked to teachers about having a dedicated staff group with lots of shared decision making and cohesion, which is exactly how the teachers responded in the pandemic crisis.

Use Information Power for Good

Part of creating a connected and safe team environment requires looking at how leaders hold or share information with teams. Leaders are often the holders of information, which is a source of power in the workplace. As discussed previously, in the absence of information, people make up often both inaccurate and fear-based stories. If leaders want to create psychological safety, there must be open and easy communication channels up, down, and sideways in their organizations. If only certain people have certain information at different times, it disrupts the creative potential of collaboration and lowers the level of trust between groups.

To differentiate between information you should share and not share is to be noticeably clear about the difference between confidential information and secret keeping or *power knowledge*. Confidential information is usually pretty clear. It is personal information people share with you in confidence or information you know because of your position of authority in the workplace. If you have knowledge of something in someone's file or a report of a child abuse investigation in a family in your school community, it is confidential. There are also times you will know the results of a decision before others due to a timeline for the announcement and to respect the parties involved (such as when retirements or new positions will be announced). Leaders are usually clear about confidentiality and know what they cannot share for legal and ethical reasons, but sometimes leaders withhold information for other reasons. These other reasons may include time concerns, secret keeping (or power knowledge), or quite frankly, just because the leaders have "always done it that way." I'll start with secret keeping.

Of the reasons for the leader to withhold information, secret keeping merits particular emphasis. *Secrets* are the things that cause you (or someone else) to close the door, look around, or lower your voice when talking, and the person confiding asks you not to say anything about it. There may be a reason secret keeping is necessary, but often the look-around or closing of the door is a sign the person is sharing something unsafe or unpopular to say publicly, and that should make you stop and question it. This concept inextricably links with power knowledge. Use the guidance in table 4.1 to help you differentiate unnecessary or unhealthy, closed communication from healthy, open communication.

Table 4.1: Traits of Closed and Open Communication

Unhealthy, Closed Communication	Healthy, Open Communication
Information that could be public is kept private.	Information is available to all.
Information is shared based on hierarchy or relationship.	Information is shared based on who needs the information for their work; the information is also available to others.
Information or decisions that may be controversial are kept quiet.	Information that may be controversial is shared as soon as possible with explanations and clarity.
A small number of people are aware of limited resources, programs, and pilots.	Everyone is aware of limited resources, programs, and pilots, and knows how and why these plans are being implemented.
Feedback is not given or is given too late.	Feedback is expected, clear, and timely.
Feedback goes only one way.	Feedback is received up and down the hierarchy and across departments.

In one school district I worked with, I noticed staff members had hoodies with the school district logo. The hoodies were beautiful and seemed popular with staff, but it looked like there were two different versions, so I asked one of the district leaders why. I could see his uncomfortable struggle to respond before he quietly closed the door and told me privately the administrators had a different version than the rest of the staff. He told me he didn't agree with the decision to have two versions because it made him uncomfortable, but some people thought it was important to use different versions. It was an interesting question on multiple levels because the leaders ordered hoodies with the district logo to create belonging and connection and as a gift to acknowledge people's hard work. Many people may not have even noticed there were two different versions. But for those who did notice, the different versions undermined their connection and sense of belonging—the very things the hoodies were designed to create.

What is even more fascinating is a senior leader, who anticipated this problem and didn't agree with this decision, didn't speak up. Why not speak up and possibly prevent a problem, or at the very least have the decision makers consider a potential problem? Also, why didn't the people who felt disconnected when they realized what had happened give feedback so their bosses could use the feedback to make a different decision next time? By not speaking up, a thoughtful gift meant to show appreciation had the opposite effect, and no one knew to do it differently next time.

"I often make a choice to pick my battles, and this one wasn't worth fighting. It has not gone over well when I have said something to this person in the past. Sometimes I can find a creative way to work it into the conversation with senior leadership for next time. They probably had no idea that it even happened because they aren't part of those details."

—District leader (personal communication, November 5, 2021)

Many leaders can probably relate to this explanation. Leaders learn to choose their battles, employ creative work-arounds, and let things go sometimes because they are worried about creating tension they would rather avoid. Research finds Canadian principals "employed subversive strategies to question entrenched power structures and transform policies, procedures, and practices that they consider counterproductive" (Wang, 2018, p. 398).

I will return to this idea of subversive leadership in chapter 5 (page 95), but for now, it is important to question some of your practices and ask whether work-arounds or letting things go is an act of resistance against unjust or unhelpful policies and practices, or just a way to avoid difficult conversations in an unsafe workplace. For example, if a leader hires someone and the usual process for posting and filling the position doesn't occur, it should be safe to ask why. There may be a great reason or the answer may be the leader is unable to explain why for some unknown reason. Either way, it should be OK to ask the question. If people stop questioning practices because it is uncomfortable or unsafe to, then it is a psychological safety issue. When people don't speak up against something they don't agree with, they are not being true to their own values and integrity, and may also be undermining the relationships they have with their coworkers.

Beware of Messaging

As a leader, you will deliver information and decisions to your teams. Hopefully, many of these decisions will relate to processes your team or staff have been involved in shaping, and you deliver the information in a timely way; there should not be big surprises. Sometimes circumstances are less than ideal, requiring leaders to make decisions quickly, but on a psychologically safe team, even when something is happening that may upset people, leaders can still deliver the message in a clear way.

Leaders should explain the thinking behind the decision and the process of arriving at the decision—and then be open to questions. (See page 94 for the reproducible, "Delivering Clear Messages.") People prefer to hear a decision they don't like over a decision or message they don't trust. This doesn't mean they will agree with or like the decision, but the relationship with and the integrity of the leader remain intact.

I can tell you about leaders I would do anything for and follow to the ends of the earth—but I can also tell you about times when I have listened to a leader deliver a message I knew was untrue. It was not the decision or the change that was difficult to adjust to; it was the betrayal of trust. I believe most of the time when people use messaging, their intention is not to mislead anyone, but rather to soften difficult messages or avoid difficult conversations. However, effective leaders must have the courage to engage in the difficult conversations and value the person and their relationships over their own comfort.

"There have been several times I have sat in a room and listened to a message I knew was not completely true. Yes, I knew the real story, but that didn't make me feel better—it just made me complicit."

—Support teacher (personal communication, October 19, 2021)

Workplace Supports and Design

Along with positive relationships, there are also different workplace supports and designs you can put in place to promote and encourage psychological safety. Once the previous structures and practices are in place, you will acquire the information you need to create these safe spaces and improve and adjust them as circumstances change. To accomplish this, leaders should: (1) ask for information and feedback and (2) embrace the messenger. These actions build and solidify trust and connection on your teams, which are essential to creating psychological safety.

Ask for Information and Feedback

Leaders ask for information and feedback regularly in a workplace that supports psychological safety (Edmondson, 2019). It is just part of how things are done. Leaders should ask for information or feedback formally at least once a year, but sharing information and feedback should also be part of the regular fabric of conversations and meetings. Doing this can be as simple as asking thoughtful and genuine questions or offering prompts and then listening to the answers. Questions and prompts may include the following.

- "Tell me more."
- "Help me understand your thinking."
- "I need your feedback on this. What do you think?"
- "This is what I am thinking, but I may be missing something, so I need your input."

Feedback can be a question or two at the end of a meeting about how the meeting went or a few questions at the end of the school year when you ask your team to help you improve and grow your leadership skills. I worked for an amazing leader who did this every year. Each year, she asked staff to answer three questions before they left on summer break.

1. "What am I doing that I need to keep doing?"
2. "What am I doing that I need to stop doing?"
3. "What am I not doing that I need to start doing?"

Sometimes feedback is difficult to hear, but it is almost always helpful. Addressing feedback is also a good way to begin the next year. The leader learned from staff and planned to incorporate that learning going forward. Giving and receiving feedback is also a big part of building trust; staff members could see the leader's genuine interest in their opinions and how she valued and used what they said to change her practice.

Create an expectation that everyone will contribute, and be clear this is not just because you want to be nice. Every voice is needed to improve the team's decision making and the valuable work the team does together. You won't use every idea you get every time, but you can make sure everyone knows you heard, considered, and valued what each person said.

In case you are worried that giving people voice is going to take all day and nothing will get done, psychological safety can and does occur in effective and efficiently run meetings. In fact, a psychologically safe meeting often means team members avoid spending a lot of time circling issues no one wants to address and instead, get things done more efficiently. The extra bonus is it is much more efficient to get things right the first time because people spoke up at the beginning and allowed ideas and corrections to surface early in the process. Sharing and being open with information take much less time than fixing things already broken or repairing damaged relationships.

Embrace the Messenger

Edmondson (2019) talks about the importance of embracing the messenger. Referencing the well-known advice to "not shoot the messenger," Edmondson (2019) says it is not enough just to leave the messenger alive; you actually must *embrace* and *reward* the person who speaks up, has the courage to bring you bad news, or questions something.

This is the behavior leaders want to reward and encourage. In addition to the prompts and questions from the previous section, try or say some of the following.

- "I am thinking this . . . but I could be wrong, so I need your input and ideas here."
- "Those are exactly the types of questions we need to move our practice forward. Thank you."
- "I never thought about it that way before; that is what is so valuable about all the different perspectives we bring. This is why we are such a great team."
- "That is really hard to hear, but I am so glad you shared it. I need a bit of time to process this, so can we take a break and come back to it? I want to give it the time and consideration it deserves." (Set a time right then to get back to it within twenty-four hours so it is not forgotten, and make sure the whole group is part of or at least hears about the follow-up.)
- After the meeting, thank the person who asked the question and tell this person the contribution is exactly the type of leadership you are looking for at this school or on this team.

As a leader, you may have to monitor your response a little if it is hard for others to hear, but take a deep breath if you need to and embrace that messenger anyway. Acknowledge it is hard for you to hear too (if you want to), but embrace the messenger's feedback with gusto!

If leaders want to create space for everyone to contribute, then when someone does have the courage to speak up about a potential problem or questions a decision or practice, leaders must show the person and everyone else listening the person made the right decision to speak up.

On the other end of the spectrum, it is also important to use *your* voice, be that brave messenger with your boss, and share your own and your team's ideas and feedback up the organizational hierarchy. I am going to pause here for a second and ask you to notice your reaction to my last sentence. Check your body response first to see how you are feeling, and then notice what you are thinking. That will give you a really good pulse on what your own workplace situation is like right now. If you felt good energy and excitement about sharing this information and wondered why I was going on about something so obvious, that is wonderful! However, if thinking about questioning decisions and practices with the people you report to fills you with dread, this is something you may want to pay more attention to.

It is important for school leaders to create safety by welcoming feedback from their own staff. But it is also important those leaders feel safe to share their considerable wisdom and the wisdom of their teams with district leadership as well. I know excellent principals and vice-principals who create safe spaces for their staff to give feedback but do not always feel safe to ask questions of their own leaders. This can create a bottleneck of information and leave the school leaders carrying an unnecessarily heavy load because they are stuck with information and unable to do anything with it. So having a safe system for feedback and questions from the school to the district level is also essential. The same strategies to create psychological safety work at all levels of the organization.

Consider the following example.

> *John is a vice-principal at a large secondary school. He has tried everything he knows to work with his principal, but it is not working. Staff are unhappy, and the stories John is hearing and the things he is witnessing do not seem OK. He also knows the district leadership team likes and respects this principal. John struggles with what to do for a long time. After consulting his mentor and then speaking directly to the principal several times, he decides to do what he thinks is the next step, and goes to the assistant superintendent about his concerns.*

How does reading this make you feel? Are you nervous for John? Do you feel like yelling, "Don't do it, John! That is career suicide"? Or are you thinking, "Well done, John! That must have been difficult, but it was absolutely the right thing to do. Your assistant superintendent must have been grateful you came to her"?

John's story could play out either way, but one thing is absolutely certain: the story impacts more than just John and his future career goals. It also impacts the behavior of everyone else who knows the story. I am not talking about the story of the principal, but the story of how the assistant superintendent treated John, as a messenger of difficult information. Did the assistant superintendent reward or punish John for speaking up?

This story then becomes the story of the school district and the template for the behavior of future leaders. What do educators want people to do in a situation like the one John found himself in? Do educators want vice-principals to stay quiet if the principal they are working for is bullying or mistreating staff? Or do they want vice-principals to do exactly what John did—even though it was difficult? How the assistant superintendent reacts to John will not only impact the behavior of everyone who knows this story but also their understanding of the school district's culture.

Leaders must create and talk about cultures of safety, where *difficult* is sometimes necessary, and leaders reward courageousness and integrity.

> *It doesn't matter what the values on the wall say, it matters how the school's values play out in staff actions and live on in the stories of those actions.*

THE FALLIBLE LEADER

If the idea of staff questioning you as leader or you questioning your own leaders has you feeling stressed, here is the good news. You were never meant to be perfect for your staff, and your leaders aren't flawless heroes either, so if you are under any illusions of that, you can just toss it all away. Educators work in a complex and dynamic system, and everyone will make mistakes sometimes. If leaders want people to be safe to try new things, they must acknowledge and celebrate mistakes, and then work with staff to fix them together.

So how do leaders do that effectively? Just spending your time correcting mistakes doesn't produce new learning and better practice, but looking at mistakes, reviewing, and reflecting on them together do (Rausch, Seifried, & Harteis, 2017). If schools are safe places to admit mistakes and reflect on them, leaders and staff can produce deeper learning and avoid quick fixes and patches that don't get at the root of the problem. So set up ways to promote learning from mistakes by being open to fallibility before it even happens (Coyle, 2018).

Leaders should start off with the humility of a learner. By acknowledging they don't know everything, and by saying things that question their own assumptions, leaders invite others to do the same. If something doesn't work out and a leader brings it to the team to reflect on and improve or change for next time, that is powerful collective learning.

Remember, leaders often learn from their interactions with their teams, both when things go well and when they don't. It is enormously powerful when you make that learning and reflection explicit. For example, consider a principal who is trying to do something kind by pulling together some fun activities for her team. She works extremely hard, spending several hours organizing the activities and treats so that responsibility doesn't fall on others, who can then just enjoy the experience. Afterward, in conversation with some of her staff members and despite the best of intentions, the principal realizes that not only did overfunctioning in this way negatively affect her own well-being, it also denied her staff (who would have loved to help) the opportunity to give back and take care of one another. Despite this "negative" outcome, because the principal went back to her team with that learning and engaged them in conversation, everyone could see one another's good intentions and planned changes for next time that would value and support everyone.

Too often in education, leaders get busy and move so quickly from initiative to initiative they forget to go back and ask if an initiative is working and adjust the plan accordingly. Of all the impacts of psychological safety, the construct it most strongly relates to is information sharing and learning (Frazier et al., 2017). If leaders create a space where it is safe to make mistakes, learn from them, and do better, that is powerful learning and exactly what educators expect students to do.

The Bottom Line

If you want to create courageous learning organizations that support your staff and ultimately your students, you need to start looking at your organization designs and structures through a well-being and psychological safety lens. At an organization level, ask questions like, "What skills and personality traits do we hire for?" "What qualities do we reward in our organization?" and "Which behaviors lead to advancement?" Leaders can create more psychological safety by how they design their workplaces at a systems level as well. This leads to the third and important (but often overlooked) part of well-being, the *system*, which I address in chapter 5 (page 95).

——— Psychological Safety Action Steps ———

1. Rebalance social power (see page 81). For example, say, "Rai, we moved through this quickly, and I know this is something you have some ideas on; did you want to add something? It would be good to hear your take on it."

2. Create collective accountability. For example, clarify everyone has the same understanding: "I just want to clarify our understanding, so we are all working together on this. Can everyone take a moment and individually write down in two sentences what problem we are trying to solve and why?" (Also see figure 4.3, page 81, for considerations when creating conditions for growth and creative solutions.)

3. Establish and expect open, clear, and timely communication (see page 85).

4. Watch for messaging (see the reproducible, "Delivering Clear Messages," on page 94).

5. Embed and embrace feedback. This can be formal or informal feedback, but do it often, and make it clear you expect it from staff. When you receive feedback, make it clear to everyone you appreciate hearing the feedback, even if it is hard to hear. For example, "This is tough feedback to hear, but it is really important, so thank you for telling me. I really want to think some more about this. Can we connect back about it tomorrow?" And then follow up the next day.

6. Review and reflect on mistakes openly and together. For example, "Well, this project had some problems for us to dig into. What did we learn, and how can we make it better next time? Some of the things I have learned are . . . ."

Delivering Clear Messages

Problem we are trying to solve:

Review of the decision-making process:
-
-
-

Acknowledge limitations, if any (that is, time, budget, ministry or district directives, and so on).

Decision:

Thinking behind the decision:
-
-
-

What we need now:

Who:

What:

When:

How, when, and where people can ask questions:

Possible questions to anticipate:
Be careful here. While it is good to prepare, it is also important to really listen to the questions and not answer based on what you anticipate the questions will be.

-
-
-

Review date: *How is it working?*

The *System*
Change Is Possible

> We do not rise to the level of our goals, we fall to the level of our systems.
>
> —James Clear

Education is a complex and multilayered system. Sometimes effecting systems change seems too difficult to tackle because the system is an impersonal, untouchable, machine-like entity seemingly out of everyone's control. I am not going to try to convince you the education system is not complex, but I do think you can and should look at how your own system's structures and practices, at both the school and district levels, impact your personal well-being and the well-being of the people on your teams. Looking at how elements of the system support or get in the way of your and your staff's well-being is an important part of the well-being triad.

It is also important to understand that increasing well-being at the systems level is not only possible but also the responsibility of an organization. The employer has a legal duty to provide a safe workplace—one where the employer avoids reasonably foreseeable harm befalling employees. Schools are increasingly applying this principle to psychological safety, as well as physical safety (Shain, 2019).

There is also an ethical responsibility of care in any social system, but especially in the education workplace. Education is an inherently relational system that goes beyond a simple exchange of goods or services—it is an interconnected relational exchange based on the ethics of care (Noddings, 2012). Organizations are not responsible for providing care, but rather for creating the environment where caring can occur. It is not enough to expect people to only take care of themselves; educators also have a responsibility to take care of one another and create conditions of care in education structures, practices, and policies (Markin & Wang, 2022).

Traditionally, people see workplaces in education systems and in the broader professional world as linear and predictable. In this view, they see the system as a set of structures, practices, and policies that the most powerful can change and control. The more I study and learn about systems, the more I agree with educator and writer Donella Meadows (2018), who describes working with systems as more of a dance, emphasizing because you can't truly control or harness systems, you have to just learn to "dance" with them. Meadows (2018) encourages people to get rid of the idea of prediction and control, and reminds them about a lesson I learn over and over again in this work: systems are beautifully messy and, as such, are a much more creative endeavor than the rigid structure many people envision. Systems are not outside entities people can control and fix. Systems are living, dynamic entities everyone is part of. Systems will always move and change, so the goal should not be to control them, but rather to design and redesign them together and with intention. As Meadows (2018) states:

> We can't impose our will upon a system. We can listen to what the system tells us, and discover how its properties and our values can work together to bring forth something much better than could ever be produced by our will alone.

With this outlook in mind, I begin this chapter with a discussion of how systems impact wellness before discussing the pitfalls of the *quick fix*. I then discuss how leaders must be clear about the systems' problems, starting by fixing the *low-hanging fruit* (problems leaders can solve with little effort) and making their actions visible. I then contemplate how to notice and name subversive leadership practices, break down big problems and ask questions, and embed structures to support well-being in education systems.

Understand How Systems Impact Well-Being

Here's an example of how the system can have an impact on well-being.

> Jaye is a mid-career, secondary teacher who is a team lead for the science department at her school. Jaye is particularly good at self-care. She knows how to do all the right things for her own health and is proud to say she practices these things fairly consistently. She eats well, sleeps well, exercises, and meditates daily.
>
> Jaye has been working at her school for several years and has developed some friendships and trust with her teammates. She has clarity about how

to contribute and feels her boss and colleagues value her. At this point in the story, things look rather good for Jaye in both the self and other parts of the triad, but how does the system fit in?

Jaye is excited about a project she is organizing with a couple of other people from different schools in the district, and she is setting up a team on the district's online platform. Jaye is not a tech expert, but she is familiar with the systems others use in her district. She is generally an early adopter of technology, so even though she has not set up a team using the district's online platform before, she is not concerned.

Sure enough, the setup looks pretty straightforward at first because there is a button that says To join or set up a team, which she clicks on. That is where she gets stuck. She can't figure out a way to set up a team. She tries a few different things, then googles for how to do it, but the instructions do not match what she sees. She connects with a friend who works with technology in the district and asks her a few questions. As it turns out, Jaye is not allowed to set up a team; teachers don't have access to do that.

Imagine for a moment you are in this situation. How are you feeling? What are you thinking? If I were Jaye, I would be frustrated and offended. I would be thinking what a waste of time it was to try to figure out the team setup myself—in addition to thinking some other, not positive thoughts about whoever set up the system. I would wonder if my leaders thought teachers were incapable or not responsible enough to do this simple task.

You can see how this sort of thinking could negatively spiral quite quickly, especially if Jaye runs into other system issues. As I already established, Jaye has the other parts of well-being going for her (notably her self-care practices), so Jaye begins using her feelings as data and reminds herself to look at other explanations.

If Jaye recognizes her frustration with this system and that making up her own explanations is not really helping her, she may choose to go to her boss, Tony, with her concerns. After all, there may be a reasonable explanation for why the system was set up that way. Tony could explain this and then fix the surface problem by setting up the online team for Jaye. Although this course of action is a quick fix for Jaye's problem, it doesn't consider or amend the *underlying inefficiency* and the *message this inefficiency sends*. The next time Jaye or one of her colleagues goes to set up a team, that teacher will run into the same problem with the same or increased levels of frustration and feelings of not being valued or trusted. Then, Tony will have to take time out of his terribly busy schedule to do a task over and over again that teachers could easily do themselves.

Another outcome is that Jaye and her colleagues simply decide not to use this online platform anymore. They may decide the old way of connecting by group email works just as well, or they may even decide not to bother connecting at all.

The latter outcome is particularly damaging given the powerful effects of professional collaboration among educators on student learning (DuFour, DuFour, Eaker, Mattos, & Muhammad, 2021).

You can see the underlying negative spiral that could happen with the quick fix. Just slowing things down long enough to wonder about a system's impact and look below the surface to the underlying problem, leaders can turn the spiral the other way.

Beware the Quick Fix

In a system already overwhelmed with competing demands for time and attention, it makes sense to look for efficient solutions to problems. But if leaders choose the quick fix, they often create only a temporary fix in the moment, not a long-term solution. This can lead to continued, time-consuming problems in the future. Instead, ask yourself, "What is the actual underlying problem?" To get at the underlying problem, be clear about what the problem is you are trying to solve. Using the previous section's example, if the problem is simply that *someone needs to create an online platform*, then Tony just creates an online team, Jaye uses it, and the problem is solved! When leaders are busy, it is tempting to keep things that simple, but when they focus only on taking care of the immediate symptom of the problem, leaders create a short-term fix that lasts only until the next occurrence.

Compassionate Systems Leadership (n.d.b) has a helpful tool for looking at this systems dilemma called *shifting the burden*. Figure 5.1 illustrates shifting the burden, which describes how you can get caught in the cycle of seeing a problem and then solving the surface issue that works in the moment. But the problem still exists, creating additional side effects. By turning your attention away from the root problem, you inadvertently make a fundamental solution difficult to achieve.

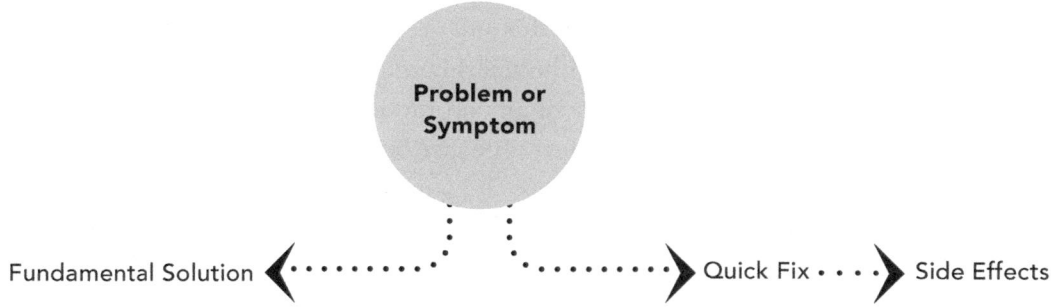

Source: Adapted from Compassionate Systems Leadership, n.d.b.

Figure 5.1: Shifting the burden.

Look at the previous example of Jaye and Tony shifting the burden, which would look something like figure 5.2.

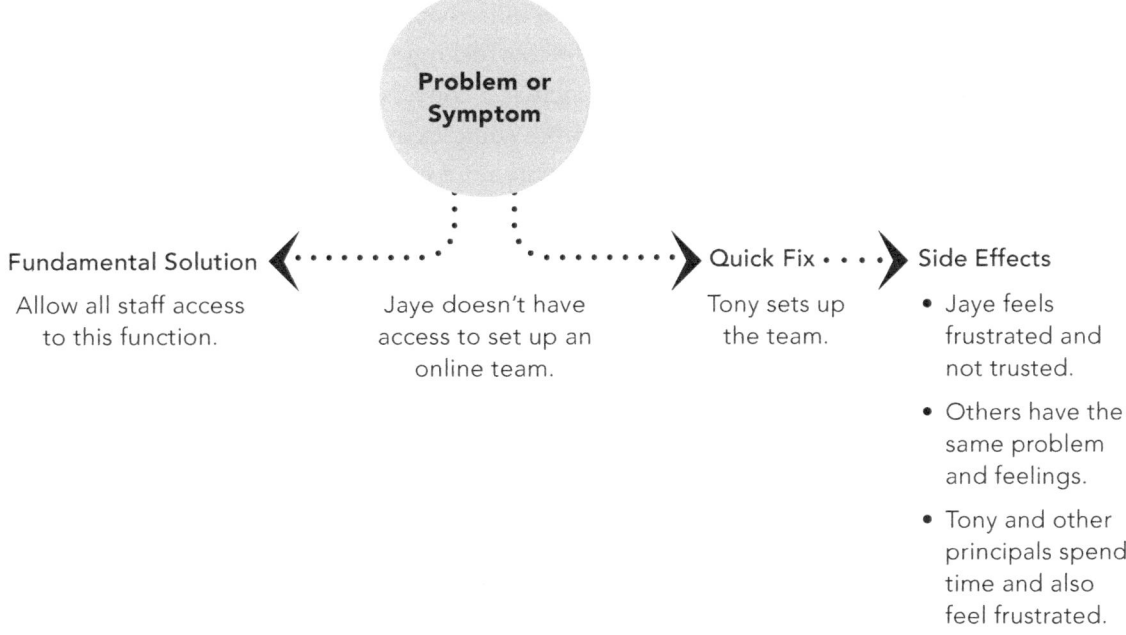

Figure 5.2: Example of Jaye and Tony shifting the burden.

This is an example of how finding a fundamental solution to an underlying problem actually takes less time than the quick fix. If you find yourself solving the same problem over and over again, you may be caught in this quick-fix cycle.

Be Clear About the Problem

To start systems change work, first be clear about the problem you are trying to solve—and the best way to do that is to ask questions. This is true of many problems leaders must work through, but it is particularly important when it comes to well-being at the systems level. Consider questions such as, What is the problem we are trying to solve? Do we all know the end goal? and Is the problem the same for everyone? Sometimes people will have a different idea about what they are trying to solve, so just coming to an agreement on the problem must come first. Maybe some people in the group are concerned about scheduling time in the gymnasium between a fun fair and basketball tournament; others think the conversation is about what educators value in the school. This leaves you, as a leader, trying to sort out how to deal with conflict among staff. All staff members might have legitimate concerns to think about, but if the goal is to work *together* to address a problem, it is vital to first clarify what the problem is.

At the systems level, leaders are not merely looking at what works for individuals but what supports the well-being of the collective. In a smaller, psychologically safe system, like a classroom or a small team, asking what the problem actually involves can be an informal process, such as a conversation about what staff or students need. However, in larger or more complex systems, like whole schools or districts, gathering data often involves the use of surveys or focus groups to determine where to consolidate efforts and resources. Both are great options for determining the most need. These two methods—(1) data-gathering via surveys and (2) data-gathering via focus groups—can also be done together, with the survey providing the quantitative population-wide data, and the focus group collecting the more qualitative data (stories and experiences).

Many excellent surveys are available to measure employee engagement, work satisfaction, and psychological health and safety. One comprehensive survey I am familiar with comes from Guarding Minds at Work (available at www.guardingmindsatwork.ca). This survey is designed to help leaders assess and address workplace psychological health and safety. The benefit of an anonymous, population-wide survey such as this is people feel free to give honest feedback when they trust their responses will not be attributed to them directly. Having population-wide data, especially over time, allows you to plan wellness initiatives that will have an impact on particular areas and also measure progress toward goals. Consider the following guidance for conducting a staff survey.

- Use a reliable and valid employee engagement and work satisfaction tool.
- Use the same survey for all staff if possible.
- Consult with and include all union groups and associations in the planning and rollout.
- Divide the results by role in the organization so everyone is represented, but only if the group is more than ten people. Groups with low numbers could be combined to provide more anonymity.
- Keep it short—twenty to thirty minutes at the longest.
- Provide time during the workday for staff to complete the survey—staff meetings often work well, especially in the beginning or in the middle of the meeting.
- If the survey is online, make sure all employees have access to the technology they need.

- If the tool is not education-specific, you should clarify some of the vocabulary on the survey before administering it. (For example, *my company* equals *my school district*.)

- Be clear you will ensure confidentiality. Often, the survey company is the only place the data are held, and the company generates a report with the results.

- Be clear about how you will use the data.

- Share the results openly within your organization.

- Provide opportunities for feedback and discussion of the results.

- Communicate to staff you will take action based on the survey results.

- Repeat the survey on a consistent timeline to track progress.

Many districts also use focus groups. Leaders gather up to ten people to discuss well-being and then categorize the information the facilitator collects into themes. The themes allow the participants to tell their story with the security of anonymity. Divide focus groups by work role—for example, one group may be elementary schoolteachers and another may be education assistants—with the aim being for each small group of up to ten people to be representative of the larger population of that group (for example, all the grade-level or schoolwide teachers or all the education assistants in a school or district). It is usually a good idea to have someone outside the district conduct the focus groups and also to have two leaders, so one person can engage in conversation and the other can record answers. (See the reproducible, "Focus Group Questions and Considerations" on page 112.) Taking time to gather the data will not be wasted; these data will give you some information about your team's strengths and problems you need to address. Data analysis allows you to focus your efforts. To access more detailed guidance on conducting focus groups, consider consulting the resources at the K–12 Staff Wellbeing BC Network (https://bc.k12wellatwork.ca) or Workplace Strategies for Mental Health (www.workplacestrategiesformentalhealth.com/resources/guarding-minds-at-work).

Start With the Low-Hanging Fruit

Once you have the data, you can quickly take action on both things that matter and things easy to do. As much as you want to avoid *only* solving the surface-level problems, that doesn't mean every solution has to be a huge, time-consuming exercise. First, simply asking a question and acknowledging you are working on an issue and thinking about systems-level well-being often create a big sigh of relief when team members realize they do not have to solve certain problems alone. There are also times when systems problems are relatively simple and easy to fix once you discover them.

My favorite example of this was when a district held focus groups and discovered the education assistants were feeling disconnected and, often, disrespected. The biggest reason they felt this way was because they didn't have a place to put their things. Other staff members had their own storage areas, but the education assistants did not. After the focus groups and in consultation with staff, the school's administrators assigned lockers to the education assistants in all the district's schools. If an education assistant worked in a particular classroom, that person's name was added to the door alongside the teacher's name. It was a simple, quick, and cost-effective fix and a powerful *belonging cue* at the same time.

After you ask questions about how people are doing and what impacts their well-being, you will probably find many opportunities for low-difficulty, high-impact actions (see the action-priority matrix in figure 5.3. The originator of this matrix is unknown). One of the biggest barriers preventing systems change is efficacy, because people think systems change is always big and takes a lot of time. If you can find quick but impactful wins, those wins go a long way toward increasing well-being, especially in the short term. In the earlier example with Tony and Jaye, the fundamental fix (opening up the system for more people to use) is just as quick and easy as the surface fix (Tony setting up the online team), but with the added bonus of not having the same problem resurface over and over again.

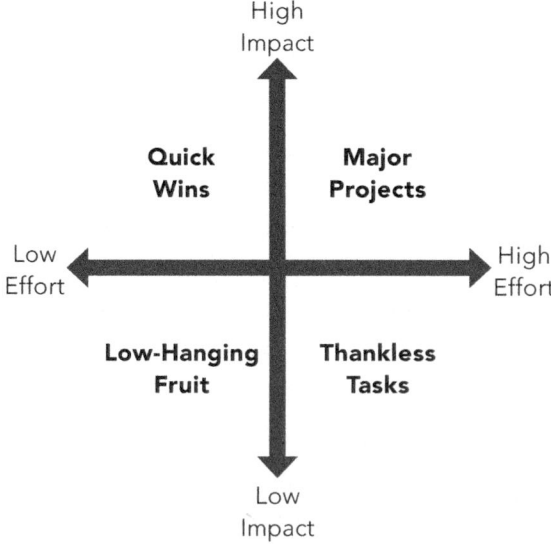

Figure 5.3: An action-priority matrix.

Make Actions Visible

Once you determine what problem you are trying to solve and find some low-hanging fruit and quick wins you can put into action easily, then you must get moving on other, longer-term projects. At the district level, this could include actions like looking at recruitment and retention practices, conducting workload reviews, or reviewing whichever area the data point you to. At the school level, this may be about finding ways to have more fun together or reviewing all the community events and extracurricular activities to determine which to focus on together with staff, so you are not attempting to address everything all at once.

No matter which actions you are working on, make sure you are talking to staff about it! It is important that people see you have heard the input they gave in the survey or focus group, and action is happening in response. Make that connection clear. This improves the efficacy of your systems change. For example, in a workplace survey I took, one of the questions asked about whether hiring and promotion decisions consider the people skills necessary for specific positions. If school district staff rated that question low effort, then an easy change would be to include criteria and questions designed to measure emotional intelligence skills in the hiring process. If human resources personnel changed their process because of the survey results, it would be helpful to let the current employees know about this change so they understand their input matters.

Explicitly discussing these small changes lets your staff see that, together, you can make systems change. Including your people in a clear process also lowers resistance to change because they see the team creating something *together*. This mindset opens up the idea of systems change and allows people to see themselves as having a responsibility for their own systems and practices. It takes away from the heroic leadership dilemma discussed previously (see page 79), where the leader is responsible for fixing everything. The system becomes less an outside, untouchable entity and more a manageable, collective responsibility.

For example, consider the following email reply one principal sent to her colleagues when they wrote to her about how long a certain task was taking:

> Thanks for your feedback on how much time the paperwork was taking, and thanks to Dean and Carla for streamlining it for us. Let's try this new draft version for the next few weeks and then check in with how it is working in case it needs tweaking. If there are any big problems, don't wait—please let me know as soon as they come up.

This example shows staff the principal heard their feedback about the excessive or inefficient paperwork and took some collective action to try and make it better. It also included the opportunity for staff to try out a new strategy to see if the changes are helpful and then provide feedback. The email was sent to all staff, making the process and solution visible, as well as creating collective responsibility for the outcome.

Notice and Name Subversive Leadership Practices

Making systems change visible is also important as a way to lower the number of subversive leadership practices in the education workplace. *Subversive leadership* is "activity that is carried out strategically to challenge and disrupt the status quo and resist policies and practices that are counterproductive to their work" (Wang, 2018, p. 398). At this point, you may wonder what's wrong with resisting counterproductive policies and practices? At a glance, perhaps nothing. But there are reasons for leaders specifically to avoid this approach to challenging systemic problems.

When people come up against a rule or practice that seems unchangeable but does not seem to be in the best interest of the students or school community, they have a tendency to "go underground." People do what makes sense according to their own ethics and values and then find a way to work around or subvert the rule (Wang, 2018). School leaders often revert to this practice because they believe they have no choice, but there are several problems with subversive leadership continuing as a long-term practice in the education system.

The first problem is that continuing to work around poor or unethical practices means those ineffective practices never change. Leaders never give them the proper scrutiny and never arrive at the "design and redesign with intention" phase the shifting the burden exercise discussed in the section, "Beware the Quick Fix" (page 98). Leaders never make the larger policy and practice changes that could create a more fundamental solution, and instead, create only a temporary solution while the problem continues. Even leaders often feel like they have no power or efficacy to impact such practices, which creates a perception that there is no choice but to work around them. Sometimes these practices have been in place so long, leaders almost don't see change as possible.

I have witnessed this effect in action with a hiring practice in my province. Leaders use only seniority to decide who is hired for posted positions. If a principal is hiring for a teaching position at her school, this practice ensures she has no choice in who gets hired. It doesn't matter how the interview goes, whether the teacher is a good fit for the school, or what other experiences and skills a candidate has, the principal *must* hire the person at the top of the seniority list.

This has been the case in many school districts in my province for such a long time that several people have told me this practice will never change. This response always surprises me because no matter whether this is an effective practice or not, it is certainly not the only way of doing things. Many school districts in other jurisdictions and even within my province hire staff differently. There is nothing unethical about this practice, but principals and teachers often work around it, so it is a practice that leaders should probably re-evaluate.

To get around this rule, many principals hold off posting open positions until other positions have been filled, the person they don't want is committed somewhere else, and the person they do *want* is at the top of the list. If that isn't possible, another strategy to subvert this rule is to post a job with extremely specific criteria to ensure only the person they want has the necessary qualifications. I understand why leaders use these strategies to work around this practice, but wouldn't it be better to simply have a conversation about why the district has this practice, and how district leaders might make their hiring practice better?

The next problem with subversive leadership is leaders feel stuck in the difficult position of having to choose between their own values and the rules and practices they are entrusted to uphold. That is a really uncomfortable and unsafe position to be in. After talking with many principals about what it is like to be in this position, researcher Fei Wang (2016) writes, "Their ethics of care becomes goodwill that enables them to engage in a certain amount of deviant behavior and express their desired identities within a role without risking too much role sanction" (p. 542). This calculated risk is deemed *worth it* for the leader to make the best decision for the student or staff member the leader is supporting.

But what are the physical, mental, and social costs to the individual making these difficult decisions? As mentioned previously, there is also a psychological-safety team cost for the leader, as rarely do these work-arounds happen without others knowing about it, and knowing about it makes them complicit. It also lowers levels of trust and creates divides on teams between the knowers and those others keep the information from. The work-arounds for the hiring practice mentioned previously are fairly well-known subversive practices that many leaders have become more comfortable with and justify as a way to hire the person who is the best fit for the school. This does sound logical and perhaps even noble until you think about the person others are trying *not* to hire. How do those candidates feel when it is happening to them? What about the principals who *do* follow the rule but are aware others do not? How do they feel? Are these leaders working in the best interest of their school by following the rules? How does this affect their relationships with their colleagues?

Don't get me wrong—I acknowledge that often a subversive leadership action is simply what needs to happen because it is the right thing to do in the moment. Subversive actions often happen when changing the system or rule is one of the bigger, more time-consuming tasks, and change will not come soon enough for the student or staff member standing in front of you. I am reminded of a story a teacher told me about when a now-retired superintendent was a principal at her school:

> I was going through a difficult divorce and on the verge of bankruptcy. I had a few days to get all the paperwork in order to finalize the divorce and all of the custody and financial agreements. I was completely on the edge of burnout and was so distracted that I felt like I wasn't able to support my students or myself and my family, so I applied for a one-week leave without pay. When human resources denied my request, I went, completely broken, to the principal. He told me to go and do what I had to do and that the school team would find a way to cover my classes. I was already a loyal employee, but after that, I would do anything for him and the team that looked after me when I needed it. (Secondary teacher, personal communication, November 8, 2021)

This is an example of when subversive leadership was the right thing to do and why I am not recommending you get rid of all subversive practices. There is no judgment here, and in fact, you can often find me celebrating the creative ways leaders find to do the right thing. My point is, leaders also need to pay attention to the uncomfortable parts and hidden downsides of subversive leadership practices, because they are important too. This all goes back to self-awareness—leaders should notice and name subversive practices and how they make them feel, so the leaders can intentionally work toward creating systems where subversions are unnecessary.

In the preceding example, the principal and the school team could have used this teacher's experience as a starting point to give some feedback about granting leaves, and then share creative solutions to support staff members when they are struggling. This could have led to change at the systems level to prevent such an event happening in the future for other staff members. I don't know what the exact right change should or could have been, but I suspect this is not the only time a situation like this occurred. In any case, if the subversive solution keeps happening, the flawed policy or practice continues to not work. Even more dangerous is that one-time solutions are inconsistent, so some may get support and others may not. What if leaders changed the policy instead? What if the conversation centered on the possibilities and the barriers?

Break Down Big Problems, Ask Questions, and Give Feedback

Some of the most important systems changes will look pretty big, but just like educators teach students, they should break these changes down into small, manageable steps. For example, when looking at staff well-being, the data often direct educators to look at human resources practices. Areas with strong union climates often lean into the "we can't do anything because of the collective agreement" argument, which ends change efforts. Stop for a moment and return to a lesson you have probably taught your students at one or many points in your career, which is to question the word *can't*.

Collective agreements are exactly as the name indicates—they are agreements administrators and educators make *together*, so of course they can and should change as the world does and as administrators and educators learn new things. That is also true of policies, practices, and rules. Educators can and *should* change all these practices as they learn, grow, and develop practices together. In the previous example, maybe the first step is for the principal to meet with human resources personnel to talk about this practice and ask questions about the reasons behind it. Sometimes there are reasons the practices or policies exist, and sometimes they need re-consideration. In the preceding example, maybe the concern was the cost of replacing the teacher. In this case, the teacher was asking for unpaid leave, and replacing that teacher with a more junior teacher would have actually saved the district money. Who knows if that was the case, but asking questions about concerns is a great first step. Maybe the next step is for the teacher to connect with the union upon returning to the school. Is this something the union wants to get on board with and renegotiate? There can be several or just a few steps afterward, but starting the process is always worth it.

Before you start to feel overwhelmed, know that as a school leader, your job is not to rework policy or renegotiate collective agreements. Your job is to *be curious*, *ask questions*, and *give the feedback necessary for that work*. The really important thing is for all leaders to support the idea that change is possible. I suspect you are now wondering that if all you are doing is supporting an idea, how does the change actually happen? *Long-term sustainable change* happens when well-being becomes so embedded in structures and systems it is just part of how you do business, part of who your organization is. I will discuss how to embed well-being in your structures and systems in the following section.

Embed Structures That Support Well-Being

Embedding well-being in a system is a beautiful and important process, but it also takes time, patience, and support. I started this chapter with Meadows's (2018) description of *systems change* as a creative dance instead of a linear system. However, even dancers require a backbone as they create and move with the music. There are some structures you can put in place to hold and support well-being and allow educators to work and create.

The first important structure is a *well-being team*. At the school or district level, this would ideally be a small team consisting of people in different roles and at different organizational levels with an interest and passion for well-being. Ideally, this team should consist of people who are willing to take off their metaphorical workday hats and work together as a group. In small schools or districts, a team may not be readily available; if that is true for you, you may need to connect across other schools or districts to find support and share ideas. I practice among a provincial community, where people across districts share ideas and resources. You can find this community of practice at Well at Work (https://k12wellatwork.ca). Visit to get some ideas. I also encourage you to find or start something similar in your area.

If you want to embed well-being into your system, it is a good idea to *bring the top leaders on board early*. Make sure district and provincial or state leaders have information about the benefits of staff well-being (see chapter 1, page 9). Keep this information short and to the point, but at the top of their minds. (See figure 5.4 for a sample letter for leaders. The statistics from "The Business Case for Well-Being," page 18, are also excellent to share.) A commitment from senior leadership allows this work to move forward much more quickly. If this commitment doesn't happen right away, be patient and keep working at whatever level of the system you have an impact on. Sharing the wins you have at a school level or the experiences of other districts can help senior leaders get a sense of what systems change can look like in practice, which can be extremely helpful.

Once you have senior leadership on board, one of the first goals of any well-being team should be to include staff well-being in the district's strategic plan. This does not need a lot of detail, but it will establish a higher-level commitment from the school or district to address staff well-being. Including staff well-being in the strategic plan makes people accountable for planning for well-being, taking action, and then measuring success. If you are working at the school level, embed staff well-being in your school plan as well. Having these structures in place will help hold space for well-being as part of the ongoing work of your team.

> [Salutation], [Name],
>
> I wanted to share some compelling information about the impact of investing in staff well-being. I know this is something that (a) *matters a great deal to you*, (b) *you are interested in*, or (c) *other reason*, and I thought it may be helpful for you to have some supporting data. Here is an infographic that lays it out clearly.
>
> [Closing],
>
> [Your name]

Figure 5.4: Example letter for leaders.

Everyone's "dance" will be different in this change, and there are no set patterns of where to put your feet, but the following are some helpful tips and ideas to consider.

- Set up a cross-role team. Consider including an administrator, a teacher, a counselor, an education assistant, and other support staff. If this is a district team, including someone from human resources is also important.
- Include someone from the local Indigenous community on the team. This brings another important well-being perspective to the group.
- Get senior leadership on board early and often.
- Include well-being in the strategic plan.
- Gather data from surveys or focus groups.
- Share these data with everyone in the organization.
- Provide time and space for input and ideas after sharing the data.
- Scan the data for high-impact and low-effort actions (quick wins), and start there.
- Make sure everyone agrees on and can clearly define the problem you are fixing.
- Beware of the surface fix and dig for the fundamental solution instead.
- Watch for subversive leadership and use evidence as data.
- Question the word *can't*.
- Do something and talk about it.

- Get feedback, review, and revise.
- Talk about what you have learned.
- Connect with others doing this work to share learning and ideas.
- Be patient, kind, and compassionate with yourself and one another.

The Bottom Line

The system part of the well-being triad may seem the most complex, but the good news is, if you have the other two parts (self and other) working, you are already making progress. Systems never stay still—they are always changing and evolving—so the important thing is to create plans with awareness and intention. Just as with the other parts of well-being, you can impact the system by noticing how things in the system make you feel, thinking through what the problem is and what you would like instead, and then taking action. The process is the same in any system, large or small. Educators just need to practice awareness and act with intention together.

System Action Steps

1. Set up a cross-role or cross-department team in your school or district or across districts.

2. Gather data from surveys or focus groups (see pages 100-101, and the reproducible, "Focus Group Questions and Considerations," page 112).

3. Get feedback on any initiatives you try, revise if necessary, and then let people know what's changed and why. For example:

    "Well, we tried the soup club, and it was fun, but with so many different lunch times, it was a bit rushed, and people who wanted to join missed out. There are some people starting a drop-in walking group that will be a fun way to connect if you are interested. The times for this group can be flexible to accommodate more schedules."

4. Create an action plan with both short- and long-term actions. Make these actions (and the *why*) visible to all. The following is a district example:

    "One of the things we learned from the focus groups is that staff not working at school sites feel out of touch with what is happening at schools and miss out on district initiatives. No matter your role, we are all working to support students together. To address this, we are now sending the district weekly update email to all staff and setting up a plan for district office staff who

are interested to visit some classrooms. Thanks for your great ideas. I can't wait to hear how it goes!"

Here is a school example:

"On the survey, one thing was really clear: we want more opportunities to connect! Connection is so important and also so much fun! One suggestion was to have a soup-and-salad club on Wednesdays at lunch. What do you think? Give that and other ideas a thought, and we can make a plan at the staff meeting on Thursday."

5. Regularly review and revise action plans as necessary. For example, review action plans every year for smaller initiatives and every two or three years for larger projects.

Focus Group Questions and Considerations

- Groups should be approximately six to ten people.
- Make sure you have enough groups so everyone is represented.
- When possible, ask for volunteers, but also consider the need for representation from different age groups, genders, grade levels, and so on, so the sample may not be random.
- Be clear about how you will maintain group anonymity.
- Consider holding the focus group offsite if possible.
- Begin the group meeting by reviewing the process and the need for confidentiality. Ensure participants know they can withdraw at any time and who the group will share the results with.
- Have two people lead the group so one person asks the questions and the other focuses on the answers.
- Record the conversation and take notes so both are available for support later.
- Provide food and a comfortable space for the group. Allow enough time for robust conversation. Two hours is a reasonable amount of time to address the four following questions (see below).
- Consider a gift to thank focus group participants for their time.

Several school districts have used the following four questions:

1. What does *well-being* mean to you?
2. What lifestyle factors promote or hinder your well-being? (Examples may include personal habits, exercise, sleep, work-life balance, and so on.)
3. What about your current system promotes or hinders your well-being?
4. What would you like to see happen within your school or district in the future to best support your well-being?

After the two group facilitators write up the themes for each question, they should share this information with the group to see if they effectively capture the conversation.

Source: Questions for schools and districts adapted from Naylor, 2019.

Conclusion

> We're going to have to learn how to listen, have hard conversations, look for joy, share pain, and be more curious than defensive, all while seeking moments of togetherness.
>
> —Brené Brown

When I think about the impact well-being can have on people and communities, I want to shout this information from the rooftops! In some ways, it just seems so simple. Slow down just a little and feel, think, and act your way to decisions that promote well-being. Because well-being impacts health, happiness, and success, it matters in every workplace, but it is especially important in education.

Education is passion work. Educators get to do amazing, impactful work that grows and shapes the next generation. It is infinitely rewarding, but it can also be exhausting and emotionally draining. Well-being is not a happy-all-the-time experience or something that will make perfect educators or leaders. That is impossible and unnecessary. Educators will always have changing emotions, and their levels of excitement and exhaustion will move up and down on any given day.

Well-being is about connecting with the passion that brought you to education in the first place and flourishing in your work as often as you can. It is about looking after yourself, caring about the people around you, and holding up one another. It is also about designing and redesigning your systems with intention and care so they support the entire learning organization's growth. Well-being is about passing the Sunday night test and going to work on Monday ready for the week ahead.

At the beginning of the book, I warned you this work takes courage. Working through the lens of well-being is simple, but not easy. It takes courage to reflect on your own practice, question established practices, and try new things. In the introduction (page 1), I invited you to feel and think your way through this book, and now it is your turn to take this learning and interaction to your practice.

I invite you to start with the guidance in chapter 1 (page 9)—the *why this matters* chapter—and share what you learned as widely as you can, so others will join in this work with you. Shout it from the rooftops with me, so others understand the potential impact of these small practices, and everyone can start moving toward well-being together.

The next step is to acknowledge the three parts of the well-being triad (self, other, and system) and start talking about how to address all three. Slow things down and move forward with intention through the three interconnected parts. Although you can address all three parts at once, it is also OK to move through each part one at a time. If you do that, it makes sense to start with yourself and then move to the belonging and connection part of *other* and finally to the *system*.

I recommend you go back to the parts of each chapter that triggered some feelings. These could not only be the parts that made you smile but also the parts that made you uncomfortable, curious, annoyed, or inspired. Start there—your best source of data about what matters most to you and probably has the most relevance in your context. The first task is just to *notice*. If something in one of the chapters resonated with you, then start noticing this in your own workplace. Just noticing what is happening and your reaction to it is an important step, so stay there for as long as you need to.

Be curious. *Being curious* includes both self-reflection and asking others for their thoughts and ideas. After feeling and thinking comes action, so look at the action steps for whichever part of well-being you are working on and try something new. Remember, working on well-being with intention should not become another thing on your to-do list, so start small and embed actions into your practice slowly. You may want to try some of the reproducible tools to help you reflect and to remind you of some of the steps you can introduce into your practice.

Above all, do this work with compassion for yourself and one another. Reflecting on practice through the lens of well-being can sometimes be uncomfortable or even downright scary because you are looking at and questioning existing practices. Be clear to all that looking at how your school or district can do things better is not a criticism of past practices or people, but an effort to improve and evolve.

Although reflection and new learning can be uncomfortable, creating well-being ultimately feels good! This beautiful and impactful work will fill your heart and soul as you watch it spread. By infusing well-being into your decision making and your practice, you impact the health, happiness, and success in your own life and in the lives of everyone around you. It really is that simple and powerful! So go out there and gently—but powerfully—change the world together!

References and Resources

Achor, S. (2018). *Big potential: How transforming the pursuit of success raises our achievement, happiness, and well-being.* New York: Currency.

Adam, E. K., Quinn, M. E., Tavernier, R., McQuillan, M. T., Dahlke, K. A., & Gilbert, K. E. (2017). Diurnal cortisol slopes and mental and physical health outcomes: A systemic review and meta-analysis. *Psychoneuroendocrinology, 83*(1), 25–41.

American Federation of Teachers, & Badass Teachers Association. (2017). *2017 educator quality of work life survey.* Accessed at www.aft.org/sites/default/files/2017_eqwl_survey_web.pdf on March 28, 2022.

Amran, A. (2022). *Ladder of inference.* Accessed at https://untools.co/ladder-of-inference on March 31, 2022.

Argyris, C. (1990). *Overcoming organizational defenses: Facilitating organizational learning.* Boston: Allyn & Bacon.

Arnold, B., Rahimi, M., & Riley, P. (2021). Working through the first year of the pandemic: A snapshot of Australian school leaders' work roles and responsibilities and health and wellbeing during COVID-19. *Journal of Educational Administration and History, 53*(3–4), 301–309.

Asamani, L., Dramanu, B. Y., & Ofosu-Amaah, E. (2020). Perception of organizational politics, psychological safety, and work efforts of senior high school teachers. *European Scientific Journal, 16*(19), 195–216.

Atasoy, R. (2020). The relationship between school principals' leadership styles, school culture and organizational change. *International Journal of Progressive Education, 16*(5), 256–274.

Barsade, S. G. (2002). The ripple effect: Emotional contagion and its influence on group behavior. *Administrative Science Quarterly, 47*(4), 644–675. Accessed at https://repository.upenn.edu/cgi/viewcontent.cgi?article=1101&context=mgmt_papers on March 28, 2022.

Baylis, L. (2021). *Self-compassion for educators: Mindful practices to awaken your well-being and grow resilience.* Eau Claire, WI: PESI.

Boell, M. M., & Senge, P. (2016, May). *School climate and social fields—An initial exploration.* Garrison, NJ: Garrison Global Collaboration for Integrative Learning. Accessed at www.garrisoninstitute.org/wp-content/uploads/2016/05/SCSF_report_revised_edition_june 2016_web_opslag.pdf on July 8, 2022.

Brackett, M. (2020). *Permission to feel: The power of emotional intelligence to achieve well-being and success.* New York: Celadon Books.

Brown, B. (2018). *Dare to lead: Brave work, tough conversations, whole hearts.* New York: Random House.

Burklund, L. J., Creswell, J. D., Irwin, M. R., & Lieberman, M. D. (2014). The common and distinct neural bases of affect labeling and reappraisal in healthy adults. *Frontiers in Psychology, 5.*

Burnett, B., & Evans, D. (2016). *Designing your life: How to build a well-lived, joyful life.* New York: Knopf.

Burton, R. (2013). Where science and story meet. *Nautilus: Science Connected.* Accessed at https://nautil.us/where-science-and-story-meet-436 on June 26, 2022.

Cable, D. M., Gino, F., & Staats, B. (2013). Breaking them in or revealing their best? Reframing socialization around newcomer self-expression. *Administrative Science Quarterly, 58*(1), 1–36. Accessed at http://nrs.harvard.edu/urn-3:HUL.InstRepos:10996793 on March 28, 2022.

Carhart-Harris, R. L., & Nutt, D. J. (2017). Serotonin and brain function: A tale of two receptors. *Journal of Psychopharmacology, 31*(9). Accessed at https://doi.org/10.1177/0269881117725915 on August 11, 2022.

Cherkowski, S., Hanson, K., & Walker, K. (2018). Flourishing in adaptive community: Balancing structures and flexibilities. *Journal of Professional Capital and Community, 3*(2), 123–136.

Cherkowski, S., Kutsyuruba, B., & Walker, K. (2020). Positive leadership: Animating purpose, presence, passion, and play for flourishing in schools. *Journal of Educational Administration, 58*(4), 401–415.

Cherkowski, S., & Walker, K. (2016). Purpose, passion and play: Exploring the construct of flourishing from the perspective of school principals. *Journal of Educational Administration, 54*(4), 378–392.

Cherkowski, S., & Walker, K. (2018). *Teacher wellbeing: Noticing, nurturing, sustaining, and flourishing in schools.* Burlington, Ontario, Canada: Word & Deed.

Chism, M. (2015). *No-drama leadership: How enlightened leaders transform culture in the workplace.* New York: Routledge.

Çiftgül, R., & Çetinkanat, A. C. (2021). The impact of school principals on teachers' organizational culture perceptions and organizational citizenship behaviors. *Revista de Cercetare și Intervenție Socială, 72,* 93–108.

Cohen, R. K., Opatosky, D. K., Savage, J., Stevens, S. O., & Darrah, E. P. (2021). *The metacognitive student: How to teach academic, social, and emotional intelligence in every content area.* Bloomington, IN: Solution Tree Press.

Collaborative for Academic, Social, and Emotional Learning. (2020, October 1). *CASEL's SEL framework.* Accessed at https://casel.org/casel-sel-framework-11-2020 on March 31, 2022.

Collinson, D., Jones, O. S., & Grint, K. (2017). "No more heroes:" Critical perspectives on leadership romanticism. *Organization Studies, 39*(11), 1625–1647.

Compassionate Systems Leadership. (n.d.a). *Check-in.* Accessed at www.compassionate systemsleadership.net/interpersonal/#checkin on October 6, 2021.

Compassionate Systems Leadership. (n.d.b). *System archetype: Shifting the burden.* Accessed at www.compassionatesystemsleadership.net/systemsthinking/#shiftingtheburden on July 8, 2022.

Coyle, D. (2018). *The culture code: The secrets of highly successful groups.* New York: Bantam Books.

Crawford, M. (2009). *Getting to the heart of leadership: Emotion and educational leadership.* London: SAGE.

Crook, N., Alakavuklar, O. N., & Bathurst, R. (2021). Leader, "know yourself": Bringing back self-awareness, trust and feedback with a theory O perspective. *Journal of Organizational Change Management, 34*(2), 350–365.

Crum, A. J., Salovey, P., & Achor, S. (2013). Rethinking stress: The role of mindsets in determining the stress response. *Journal of Personality and Social Psychology, 104*(4), 716–733.

Curhan, J. R., & Pentland, A. (2007). Thin slices of negotiation: Predicting outcomes from conversational dynamics within the first 5 minutes. *Journal of Applied Psychology, 92*(3), 802–811. Accessed at https://psycnet.apa.org/doiLanding?doi=10.1037%2F0021-9010.92.3.802 on July 18, 2022.

Deloitte Insights. (2019). *The ROI in workplace mental health programs: Good for people, good for business—A blueprint for workplace mental health programs.* Accessed at www2.deloitte.com/content/dam/Deloitte/ca/Documents/about-deloitte/ca-en-about-blueprint-for-workplace-mental-health-final-aoda.pdf on July 8, 2022.

Detert, J., & Bruno, E. (2021, Summer). The courage to be candid. *MIT Sloan Management Review.* Accessed at https://sloanreview.mit.edu/article/the-courage-to-be-candid on July 18, 2022.

Dimant, E. (2019). Contagion of pro- and anti-social behavior among peers and the role of social proximity. *Journal of Economic Psychology, 73,* 66–88.

DuFour, R., DuFour, R., Eaker, R., Mattos, M., & Muhammad, A. (2021). *Revisiting PLCs at Work: Proven insights for sustained, substantive school improvement* (2nd ed.). Bloomington, IN: Solution Tree Press.

Duhigg, C. (2016, February 25). What Google learned from its quest to build the perfect team. *The New York Times Magazine.* Accessed at www.nytimes.com/2016/02/28/magazine/what-google-learned-from-its-quest-to-build-the-perfect-team.html on June 27, 2022.

Dunbar, R. I. M. (1993). Coevolution of neocortical size, group size and language in humans. *Behavioral and Brain Sciences, 16*(4), 681–694.

Durlak, J. A., Weissberg, R. P., Dymnicki, A. B., Taylor, R. D., & Schellinger, K. B. (2011). The impact of enhancing students' social and emotional learning: A meta-analysis of school-based universal interventions. *Child Development, 82*(1), 405–432. Accessed at www.jstor.org/stable/29782838 on April 5, 2021.

Eby, L. T. D. T., & Allen, T. D. (Eds.). (2012). *Personal relationships: The effect on employee attitudes, behavior, and well-being.* New York: Routledge.

EdCan Network. (n.d.). *K–12 staff stress and burnout: An issue worthy of investment*. Accessed at https://edcan.ca/wp-content/uploads/Final-_Infographic-_-K12StaffStressAndBurnout_Well AtWork_EdCan.pdf on March 29, 2022.

EdCan Network. (2021, January 11). *Testing and adapting two innovative approaches to workplace wellbeing in K–12 education*. Accessed at https://edcannetwork.wordpress.com/2021/01/11 /practitioner-report on June 26, 2022.

Edmondson, A. C. (2019). *The fearless organization: Creating psychological safety in the workplace for learning, innovation, and growth*. Hoboken, NJ: Wiley.

Edmondson, A. C., Higgins, M., Singer, S., & Weiner, J. (2016). Understanding psychological safety in health care and education organizations: A comparative perspective. *Research in Human Development, 13*(1), 65–83.

Edmondson, A. C., & Lei, Z. (2014). Psychological safety: The history, renaissance, and future of an interpersonal construct. *Annual Review of Organizational Psychology and Organizational Behavior, 1*(1), 23–43.

Eisenberger, N. I. (2012). The pain of social disconnection: Examining the shared neural underpinnings of physical and social pain. *Nature Reviews Neuroscience, 13*(6), 421–434.

Eisenberger, N. I., & Lieberman, M. D. (2004). Why rejection hurts: A common neural alarm system for physical and social pain. *Trends in Cognitive Sciences, 8*(7), 294–300.

Eisenberger, N. I., Lieberman, M. D., & Williams, K. D. (2003). Does rejection hurt? An FMRI study of social exclusion. *Science, 302*(5643), 290–292.

The Eurich Group. (2022). *The insight quiz*. Accessed at www.insight-book.com/quiz on March 31, 2022.

Eurich, T. (2017). *Insight: Why we're not as self-aware as we think, and how seeing ourselves clearly helps us succeed at work and in life*. New York: Crown Business.

Eurich, T. (2019). What self-awareness really is (and how to cultivate it). In *Emotional intelligence: Self awareness* (pp. 11–35). Boston: Harvard Business Review Press.

Fiester, A. (2022, April 18). The "ladder of inference" as a conflict management tool: Working with the "difficult" patient or family in healthcare ethics consultations. *HEC Forum*. Accessed at https://pubmed.ncbi.nlm.nih.gov/35435533/ on October 6, 2022.

Frazier, M. L., Fainshmidt, S., Klinger, R. L., Pezeshkan, A., & Vracheva, V. (2017). Psychological safety: A meta-analytic review and extension. *Personnel Psychology, 70*(1), 113–165.

Froese-Germain, B. (2014, July). *Work-life balance and the Canadian teaching profession*. Ottawa, Ontario, Canada: Canadian Teachers' Federation. Accessed at https://files.eric.ed.gov/fulltext/ED546884.pdf on March 28, 2022.

Gabriel, S. (2020). Reflections on the 25th anniversary of Baumeister and Leary's seminal paper on the need to belong. *Self and Identity, 20*(1), 1–5.

Grace, S. A., Rossell, S. L., Heinrichs, M., Kordsachia, C., & Labuschagne, I. (2018). Oxytocin and brain activity in humans: A systematic review and coordinate-based meta-analysis of functional MRI studies. *Psychoneuroendocrinology, 96*, 6–24. Accessed at https://doi.org/10.1016/j.psyneuen.2018.05.031 on August 11, 2022.

Greenbaum, R. L., Bonner, J. M., Mawritz, M. B., Butts, M. M., & Smith, M. B. (2020). It is all about the bottom line: Group bottom-line mentality, psychological safety, and group creativity. *Journal of Organizational Behavior, 41*(6), 503–517.

Greenberg, M. T., Brown, J. L., & Abenavoli, R. M. (2016). *Teacher stress and health: Effects on teachers, students, and schools.* State College: Edna Bennett Pierce Prevention Research Center, Pennsylvania State University. Accessed at www.prevention.psu.edu/uploads/files/rwjf430428-TeacherStress.pdf on October 6, 2022.

Hanson, R. (2018). *Resilient: How to grow an unshakable core of calm, strength, and happiness.* New York: Harmony Books.

Harris, R. (2019). *ACT made simple: An easy-to-read primer on acceptance and commitment therapy* (2nd ed.). Oakland, CA: New Harbinger.

Hedges, K. (2019). How are you perceived at work? Here's an exercise to find out. In *Emotional intelligence: Self-awareness* (pp. 109–117). Boston: Harvard Business Review Press.

Holt-Lunstad, J., Smith, T. B., & Layton, J. B. (2010). Social relationships and mortality risk: A meta-analytic review. *PLoS Medicine, 7*(7). Accessed at https://pubmed.ncbi.nlm.nih.gov/20668659 on March 30, 2022.

Hudd, T., & Moscovitch, D. A. (2020). Coping with social wounds: How social pain and social anxiety influence access to social rewards. *Journal of Behavior Therapy and Experimental Psychiatry, 68*, 101572.

Hudd, T., & Moscovitch, D. A. (2021). Social pain and the role of imagined social consequences: Why personal adverse experiences elicit social pain, with or without explicit relational devaluation. *Journal of Experimental Social Psychology, 95*, 104121. Accessed at www.sciencedirect.com/science/article/abs/pii/S0022103121000214?via%3Dihub on July 8, 2022.

Hutchison, S. M., Watts, A., Gadermann, A., Oberle, E., Oberlander, T. F., Lavoie, P. M., et al. (2021). School staff and teachers during the second year of COVID-19: Higher anxiety symptoms, higher psychological distress, and poorer mental health compared to the general population. *Journal of Affective Disorders Reports, 8*, 100335. Accessed at www.sciencedirect.com/science/article/pii/S2666915322000282 on July 5, 2022.

K–12 Staff Wellbeing BC Network. (n.d.). *Our approach.* Accessed at https://bc.k12wellatwork.ca/our-approach on July 5, 2022.

Kasos, E., Kasos, K., Pusztai, F., Polyák, Á., Kovács, K. J., & Varga, K. (2018). Changes in oxytocin and cortisol in active-alert hypnosis: Hormonal changes benefiting low hypnotizable participants. *International Journal of Clinical and Experimental Hypnosis, 66*(4), 404–427.

Larson, E., & Jivapong, B. (2021). *Reach out: An employer's guide to using behavioral insights in supporting staff mental health and wellbeing.* Accessed at www.bi.team/wp-content/uploads/2021/01/Mental-Health-Guide.pdf on June 26, 2022.

Lieberman, M. D. (2013). *Social: Why our brains are wired to connect.* New York: Broadway Books.

Lindenfors, P., Wartel, A., & Lind, J. (2021). "Dunbar's number" deconstructed. *Biology Letters, 17*(5), 1–4. Accessed at https://royalsocietypublishing.org/doi/10.1098/rsbl.2021.0158 on July 7, 2022.

Lohaus, D., & Habermann, W. (2019). Presenteeism: A review and research directions. *Human Resource Management Review, 29*(1), 43–58.

Mahfouz, J. (2018). Mindfulness training for school administrators: Effects on well-being and leadership. *Journal of Educational Administration, 56*(6), 602–619.

Mahoney, J. L., Durlak, J. A., & Weissberg, R. P. (2018). An update on social and emotional learning outcome research. *Phi Delta Kappan, 100*(4), 18–23.

Mann, A. (2018, January 15). *Why we need best friends at work.* Accessed at www.gallup.com/workplace/236213/why-need-best-friends-work.aspx on February 28, 2021.

Markin, G. (2019, April). *The secret to health, happiness and success together* [Video file]. Accessed at www.ted.com/talks/gail_markin_the_secret_to_health_happiness_and_success_together/up-next on March 28, 2022.

Markin, G., & Wang, F. (2022). Well-being: An ethical responsibility for educational organizations. In I. A. Marshall, G.-A. Jackman, & D. E. Armstrong (Eds.), *The early years of leadership: The journey begins* (pp. 199–214). Charlotte, NC: Information Age.

Marsh, N., Marsh, A. A., Lee, M. R., & Hurlemann, R. (2021). Oxytocin and the neurobiology of prosocial behavior. *The Neuroscientist: A Review Journal Bringing Neurobiology, Neurology and Psychiatry, 27*(6), 604–619. Accessed at https://doiorg/10.1177/1073858420960111 on August 11, 2022.

Mazurek, K. A., & Schieber, M. H. (2019). Mirror neurons precede non-mirror neurons during action execution. *Journal of Neurophysiology, 122*(6), 2630–2635. Accessed at https://journals.physiology.org/doi/full/10.1152/jn.00653.2019 on July 8, 2022.

Meadows, D. (2018). *Dancing with systems.* Accessed at https://thesystemsthinker.com/dancing-with-systems on March 28, 2022.

Mental Health Commission of Canada. (n.d.). *National Standard.* Accessed at https://mentalhealthcommission.ca/national-standard on July 7, 2022.

Michael, M. (2022). *From burnt out to fired up: Reigniting your passion for teaching.* Bloomington, IN: Solution Tree Press.

Montemurro, G., Storey, K., Cherkowski, S., Sulz, L., Saville, L., & Loland, D. (in press). *Prioritizing well-being in K–12 education: Lessons from a multiple case study of Canadian school districts.*

Mulder, P. (2018). *Ladder of inference (Argyris & Senge).* Accessed at www.toolshero.com/decision-making/ladder-of-inference on March 31, 2022.

Nagoski, E., & Nagoski, A. (2018, December). BURNOUT: The secret to unlocking the stress cycle. *Library Journal, 143*(20), 17A. Accessed at https://link.gale.com/apps/doc/A564606927/LitRC?u=ubcolumbia&sid=summon&xid=5eafcfbe on March 28, 2022.

Naylor, C. (2019, September 18). *Staff well-being in schools: Some B.C. ideas and approaches.* Accessed at https://k12wellatwork.ca/article-series/staff-well-being-in-schoolsgroup on March 31, 2022.

Nembhard, I. M., & Edmondson, A. C. (2006). Making it safe: The effects of leader inclusiveness and professional status on psychological safety and improvement efforts in health care teams. *Journal of Organizational Behavior, 27*(7), 941–966.

Noddings, N. (2012). The caring relation in teaching. *Oxford Review of Education, 38*(6), 771–781.

Oberle, E., & Schonert-Reichl, K. A. (2016). Stress contagion in the classroom? The link between classroom teacher burnout and morning cortisol in elementary school students. *Social Science and Medicine, 159*, 30–37.

Pollock, K. (2014, September). *The changing nature of principals' work: Final report.* Toronto, Ontario, Canada: Ontario Principals' Council.

Pollock, K. (2017, June). *The changing nature of vice-principals' work: Final report.* Toronto, Ontario, Canada: Ontario Principals' Council.

Porosoff, L., & Weinstein, J. (2023). *EMPOWER moves for social-emotional learning: Tools and strategies to evoke student values.* Bloomington, IN: Solution Tree Press.

Poulou, M. S. (2017). Students' emotional and behavioral difficulties: The role of teachers' social and emotional learning and teacher-student relationships. *International Journal of Emotional Education, 9*(2), 72–89.

Poulou, M. S. (2018). Students' emotional and behavioral difficulties: The role of teachers' social and emotional learning and teacher-student relationships—Postscript. *International Journal of Emotional Education, 10*(2), 146–153.

Province of British Columbia. (n.d.). *Curriculum redesign: Introduction to BC's curriculum redesign.* Accessed at https://curriculum.gov.bc.ca/rethinking-curriculum on July 8, 2022.

Rao, A. R. (2018). An oscillatory neural network model that demonstrates the benefits of multisensory learning. *Cognitive Neurodynamics, 12*, 481–499.

Rausch, A., Seifried, J., & Harteis, C. (2017). Emotions, coping and learning in error situations in the workplace. *Journal of Workplace Learning, 29*(5), 370–389. Accessed at https://researchgate.net/publication/318228404_Emotions_coping_and_learning_in_error_situations_in_the_workplace on March 28, 2022.

Ricœur, P. (1992). *Oneself as another* (K. Blamey, Trans.). Chicago: University of Chicago Press.

Russell, G., & Lightman, S. (2019). The human stress response. *Nature Reviews: Endocrinology, 15*(9), 525–534. Accessed at https://link.gale.com/apps/doc/A596089774/HRCA on March 28, 2022.

Sandvik, A. M., Gjevestad, E., Aabrekk, E., Øhman, P., Kjendlie, P., Hystad, S. W., et al. (2020). Physical fitness and psychological hardiness as predictors of parasympathetic control in response to stress: A Norwegian police simulator training study. *Journal of Police and Criminal Psychology, 35*, 504–517.

Schlegel, D., & Parascando, J. (2020). What's happening in your head: Overcoming our assumptions to work better together. *MedEdPORTAL: The AAMC Journal of Teaching and Learning Resources, 16.* Accessed at www.mededportal.org/doi/pdf/10.15766/mep_2374-8265.11034 on March 28, 2022.

Schmidt, B., Schneider, M., Seeger, P., van Vianen, A., Loerbroks, A., & Herr, R. M. (2019). A comparison of job stress models: Associations with employee well-being, absenteeism, presenteeism, and resulting costs. *Journal of Occupational and Environmental Medicine, 61*(7), 535–544.

Schonert-Reichl, K. A. (2017). Social and emotional learning and teachers. *The Future of Children*, *27*(1), 137–155.

Seligman, M. E. P. (2011). *Flourish: A visionary new understanding of happiness and well-being*. New York: Free Press.

Senge, P., Cambron-McCabe, N., Lucas, T., Smith, B., Dutton, J., & Kleiner, A. (2012). *Schools that learn: A fifth discipline fieldbook for educators, parents, and everyone who cares about education* (1st rev. ed.). New York: Crown Business.

Shain, M. (2019, August). *Getting ahead of the perfect legal storm: Toward a basic legal standard of care for workers' psychological safety*. Accessed at https://wsmh-cms.mediresource.com/wsmh/assets/jkmww6y57fccc80s on December 5, 2021.

Sheerha, A., & Singhvi, M. (2016). How does positive visualization affect people's level of happiness and perception of their physical body image? *Indian Journal of Positive Psychology*, *7*(4), 472–479.

Shields-Lysiak, L. K., Boyd, M. P., Iorio, J. P., Jr., & Vasquez, C. R. (2020). Classroom greetings: More than a simple hello. *Iranian Journal of Language Teaching Research*, *8*(3), 41–56.

Sinek, S. (2014). *Leaders eat last: Why some teams pull together and others don't*. New York: Portfolio/Penguin.

Smither, J. W., London, M., Vasilopoulos, N. L., Reilly, R. R., Millsap, R. E., & Salvemini, N. (1995). An examination of the effects of an upward feedback program over time. *Personnel Psychology*, *48*(1), 1–34. Accessed at https://proquest.com/scholarly-journals/examination-effects-upward-feedback-program-over/docview/220134257/se-2?accountid=14656 on March 28, 2022.

Statistics Canada. (2019). *Daily average time spent in hours on various activities by age group and sex, 15 years and over, Canada and provinces*. Accessed at www150.statcan.gc.ca/t1/tbl1/en/tv.action?pid=4510001401 on March 28, 2022.

Sy, T., & Choi, J. N. (2013). Contagious leaders and followers: Exploring multi-stage mood contagion in a leader activation and member propagation (LAMP) model. *Organizational Behavior and Human Decision Processes*, *122*(2), 127–140.

Taylor, R. D., Oberle, E., Durlak, J. A., & Weissberg, R. P. (2017). Promoting positive youth development through school-based social and emotional learning interventions: A meta-analysis of follow-up effects. *Child Development*, *88*(4), 1156–1171.

Tolle, E. (2005). *A new earth: Awakening to your life's purpose*. New York: Dutton/Penguin.

Van Swol, L. M., & Kane, A. A. (2018). Language and group processes: An integrative, interdisciplinary review. *Small Group Research*, *50*(1), 3–38.

Verkuil, B., Brosschot, J. F., Meerman, E. E., & Thayer, J. F. (2010). Effects of momentary assessed stressful events and worry episodes on somatic health complaints. *Psychology and Health*, *27*(2), 141–158.

Verkuil, B., Brosschot, J. F., Tollenaar, M. S., Lane, R. D., & Thayer, J. F. (2016). Prolonged non-metabolic heart rate variability reduction as a physiological marker of psychological stress in daily life. *Annals of Behavioral Medicine: A Publication of the Society of Behavioral Medicine*, *50*(5), 704–714.

Wang, F. (2016). Leadership as a subversive activity: Principals' perceptions. *International Journal of Leadership in Education*, *21*(5), 531–544.

Wang, F. (2018). Subversive leadership and power tactics. *Journal of Educational Administration*, *56*(4), 398–413.

Wang, F., & Pollock, K. (2020). *Principals' work and well-being in British Columbia: Infographic booklets.* Accessed at https://edst-educ.sites.olt.ubc.ca/files/2020/07/UBC-Principals-Work-Infographic-Booklets-Links.pdf on March 28, 2022.

Wang, F., Pollock, K., & Hauseman, C. (2018). School principals' job satisfaction: The effects of work intensification. *Canadian Journal of Educational Administration and Policy*, *185*, 73–90.

Wang, F., Pollock, K., & Hauseman, C. (2021). Complexity and volume: Work intensification of vice-principals in Ontario. *International Journal of Leadership in Education.* Accessed at www.tandfonline.com/doi/full/10.1080/13603124.2021.1974097 on October 6, 2022.

Weiner, J., Francois, C., Stone-Johnson, C., & Childs, J. (2021). Keep safe, keep learning: Principals' role in creating psychological safety and organizational learning during the COVID-19 pandemic. *Frontiers in Education.* Accessed at www.frontiersin.org/articles/10.3389/feduc.2020.618483/full on October 6, 2022.

Wellman, B. (2012). Is Dunbar's number up? *The British Journal of Psychology*, *103*(2), 174–176.

Wisniewski, R., & Foster, L. R. (2020, October 27–30). *Addressing the social-emotional needs of adult learners to ensure workplace success: Combined practices that integrate social emotional learning and employability skills.* Presented online at the American Association for Adult and Continuing Education 2020 conference.

Yang, Y., Li, Z., Liang, L., & Zhang, X. (2021). Why and when paradoxical leader behavior impact employee creativity: Thriving at work and psychological safety. *Current Psychology*, *40*, 1911–1922.

Zell, E., & Križan, Z. (2014). Do people have insight into their abilities? A metasynthesis. *Perspectives on Psychological Science*, *9*(2), 111–125.

Index

A

absenteeism
    business case for well-being and, 19
    traditional approach to self-care and, 24
acting and components of human behavior, 4
action-priority matrix, 102
actions, visibility of, 103–104
adrenaline, 14–16
Alakavuklar, O., 78–79
American Federation of Teachers and Badass Teachers Association, 2
arousal, heightened states of, 14, 15–16
attendance support programs, 24

B

Bathurst, R., 78–79
beauty of and problems with self-care. *See* self-care
behavior, components of human behavior, 4
belonging. *See also* social connection and belonging
    about, 47–49
    mirror neurons and, 49–50
    serotonin and oxytocin and, 50–52
    well-being and, xiv
belonging cues
    about, 54–56
    examples of how identifying negativity bias and determining possible actions and belonging cues helps leaders respond to situations, 65
    low-hanging fruit and, 102
Brown, B., 63–64
burnout
    bandages on the elephant and, 25–26
    business case for well-being and, 19
    stress and, 15, 19

C

care
    placing value on care, collegiality, collaboration, and collective accountability, 83–84
    systems and, 95–96
check-ins, 58
circle of safety, 73. *See also* psychological safety
classroom practices, 77–78
collaboration, placing value on, 83–84
collective accountability, placing value on, 83–84
collective agreements, 107
collegiality, placing value on, 83–84
communication
    information power and, 84–86

traits of closed and open communication, 85
ways to share effective self-care practices and, 29
compassionate systems leadership, 57–58
confidentiality, 84
connection and well-being, xiv. *See also* belonging cues
cortisol
    contagion effect and, 17
    oxytocin and, 53
    stress response cycle and, 14
COVID-19
    positive leader relations and, 83
    simple and personal messages during, 29
    stress and, 2
creating conditions for growth and creative solutions, 81. *See also* psychological safety
Crook, N., 78–79
curiosity, 114
cycle of safety, 72. *See also* psychological safety

D

data-gathering
    clarity about the problem and, 100–101
    well-being teams and, 109
Dunbar number, 56–57

E

Edmondson, A., 76, 89
emotions. *See also* feelings
    contagion effect and, 17
    emotional pain, 48
    labeling, 32
    self-awareness and, 10, 31, 33
energy and belonging cues, 54
Eurich, T., 30
external self-awareness practices, 36, 38–39. *See also* self-awareness

F

face-to-face interactions, 56–57
fallibility of leaders, 91–92
feedback
    actions, visibility of, 103
    breaking down big problems, asking questions, and giving feedback, 107
    data-gathering and, 100
    external self-awareness practices and, 38–39
    hierarchy of the system and, xiv
    workplace supports and designs and, 88–89
feelings. *See also* emotions
    and the body, 13
    and components of human behavior, 4
    and contagion effect, 54
    and self-awareness, 31–33
    and SELF-care tools, 5
    and self-management, 10
    and social-emotional learning, 11
flourishing, promoting by connecting to passion, 59–60
focus groups
    data-gathering and, 100–101
    well-being teams and, 109
formal leadership and rebalancing social power, 81, 82. *See also* leadership
friendship
    impact of, 59
    oxytocin and, 51
future orientation, 55

H

Hanson, R., 63
health promotions, 24–25
heightened states of arousal, 14, 15–16

heroic leadership, 79, 103. *See also* leadership
hierarchy, 61–62

I

Indigenous voices, 62, 109
individualism and belonging cues, 55
informal leadership and rebalancing social power, 81, 82. *See also* leadership
information power, 84–86
Insight: Why We're Not as Self-Aware as We Think, and How Seeing Ourselves Clearly Helps Us Succeed at Work and in Life (Eurich), 30
internal self-awareness practices. *See also* self-awareness
    about, 31
    ladder of inference and, 34–36, 37
    notice, label, act and, 31–34
introduction
    about this book, 4–7
    about well-being, 1
    why educators are not all right, 2–3
    why I wrote this book, 3–4

L

ladder of inference, 34–36, 37
leadership. *See also* positive leader relations
    fallibility of, 91–92
    heroic leadership, 79, 103
    leading with relationships, 56–58
    rebalancing social power and, 81–83
    self-care and, 23
Lei, Z., 76
Lieberman, M., 47
love hormone. *See* oxytocin

M

Meadows, D., 96

meditation script example, 58
meetings
    belonging cues and, 56
    check-ins and, 58
    making connections explicit and, 59
    negativity bias and inaccurate stories and, 63
    psychological safety and, 88–89
    rebalancing social power and, 82, 83
messaging
    beware of messaging, 86–87
    and understanding how systems impact well-being, 97
    and ways to share effective self-care practices, 29
messengers, embracing, 89–91
mirror neurons, 49–50

N

Nagoski, A., 15
Nagoski, E., 15
negative emotions, 17. *See also* emotions
negativity bias and inaccurate stories, 63–64
nervous system stress responses
    contagion effect and, 17–18
    sympathetic nervous system and, 14–17
neurons, mirror, 49–50
neurotransmitters, 50–52
notice, label, act, 31–34
noticing activities, 60

O

othering, 61–62
others. *See also* psychological safety; social connection and belonging
    example of ways to acknowledge all three parts of well-being, 28

and interconnected parts of well-being, 5
and self-care, 26
oxytocin
    belonging and, 51–52
    cortisol and, 53

P

pain, social pain, 47–48
passion, promoting flourishing by connecting to passion, 59–60
physical pain, 48
positive leader relations. *See also* leadership
    about, 79–80
    information power and, 84–86
    messaging and, 86–87
    placing value on care, collegiality, collaboration, and collective accountability and, 83–84
    rebalancing social power and, 81–83
positive visualizations, 32
power, social power, 81–83
power knowledge, 84
presenteeism, 18–19
principals and why I wrote this book, 4
promoting flourishing by connecting to passion, 59–60
psychological safety
    about, 71–72
    action steps for, 92–93
    bottom line for, 92
    fallibility of leaders and, 91–92
    positive leader relations and, 79–87
    psychological safety, defined, 76–91
    psychologically safe workplace, 72–76
    reproducibles for, 94
    workplace supports and designs, 87–91

Psychological Safety: The History, Renaissance, and Future of an Interpersonal Construct (Edmondson and Lei), 76
pulling the alarm code, 64

Q

quick fixes, beware of, 98–99
quick wins
    low-hanging fruit and, 101–102
    well-being teams and, 109

R

rebalancing social power, 81–83
rejection, 47–48
relationships
    impact of, 46
    leading with, 56–58
    positive leader relations, 79–87
    relationship-based workplaces, 52–54
    social-emotional learning and, 10
reproducibles for
    check-in protocol for building self-awareness, team connection, and belonging, 67
    delivering clear messages, 94
    focus group questions and considerations, 112
    identifying negativity bias and determining actions and belonging cues, 70
    protocol for appreciative inquiry, 68–69
    steps to build and use self-awareness, 41–43
    steps to build external self-awareness, 44
responsible decision making, 10
Ricœur, P., 10

S

secrets, 84–85

self
- beauty of and problems with self-care. *See* self-care
- example of ways to acknowledge all three parts of well-being, 28
- and interconnected parts of well-being, 5

self-awareness
- about, 30–31
- external self-awareness practices, 36, 38–39
- internal self-awareness practices, 31–36
- leading with relationships and, 57–58
- self-care and, 30–39
- social-emotional learning and, 10

self-care
- about, 23
- action steps for, 40
- bandages on the elephant and, 25–26
- bottom line for, 39
- reproducibles for, 41–44
- traditional approaches to, 23–25
- ways to share effective self-care practices, 26–30

SELF-care tools, 5
self-management, 10, 30
serotonin and oxytocin, 50–52
shifting the burden, 98–99
Sinek, S., 9–10
social awareness, 10
social connection and belonging. *See also* belonging
- about, 45–46
- action steps for, 66
- belonging cues and action strategies, 54–60
- bottom line for, 64
- culture of connection, not competition and, 60–62
- need to belong and, 47–52
- negativity bias and inaccurate stories and, 63–64
- relationship-based workplaces and, 52–54
- reproducibles for, 67–70

social pain, 47–48
social power, 81–83
Social: Why Our Brains Are Wired to Connect (Lieberman), 47
social-emotional learning (SEL)
- self-care and, 29–30
- well-being and, 10–12

sociometer, 56
soft skills, 3, 11
story-building, stages of, 34
strategies for social connection and belonging
- about, 54–56
- leading with relationships, 56–58
- making connections explicit, 59
- promoting flourishing by connecting to passion, 59–60

stress
- bandages on the elephant and, 25–26
- contagion effect and, 17–18
- human body and, 13–18
- impact of, 19
- stress response cycle, 14–17
- why educators are not all right, 2–3

stress leaves, 23–24
stress response cycle
- about, 14–18
- notice, label, act and, 33

subversive leadership
- about, 104–106
- information power and, 86
- psychological safety and, 78
- well-being teams and, 109

Sunday night test, 2
surface problems, 97

surveys
- data-gathering and, 100–101
- well-being teams and, 109

systems
- about, 95–96
- action steps for, 110–111
- actions, visibility of, 103–104
- bottom line for, 110
- breaking down big problems, asking questions, and giving feedback, 107
- clarity about the problem and, 99–101
- embedding structures that support well-being and, 108–110
- example of ways to acknowledge all three parts of well-being, 28
- interconnected parts of well-being and, 5, 6
- low-hanging fruit and, 101–102
- quick fixes, beware of, 98–99
- reproducibles for, 112
- self-care and, 26
- subversive leadership and, 104–106
- understanding how systems impact well-being, 96–98

T

teams, well-being teams, 108–110
thinking and components of human behavior, 4

U

unsafe cycles, 74. *See also* psychological safety

V

values, four features of, 34

W

waterfall chats, 82
Weiner, J., 83
well-being
- about, 1
- business case for, 18–20
- embedding structures that support, 108–110
- example of ways to acknowledge all three parts of, 28
- importance of, xiii
- interconnected parts of, 5–6
- soft skills and, 3
- systems and, 96–98
- why, the. *See* why well-being matters

well-being teams, 108–110
wellness programs, traditional approach to, 23–25
why well-being matters
- about, 9–10
- action steps for well-being, 21
- bottom line for, 20
- business case for well-being, 18–20
- health, happiness, and success at work and, 13–18
- social-emotional learning and well-being, 10–12

work environment
- psychological safety, defined, 77–78
- psychologically safe workplace, 72–76
- workplace supports and designs, 87–91

Y

yoga Fridays, 57

180 Days of Self-Care for Busy Educators
Tina H. Boogren

Rely on *180 Days of Self-Care for Busy Educators* to help you lead a happier, healthier, more fulfilled life inside and outside of the classroom. With Tina H. Boogren's guidance, you will work through 36 weeks of self-care strategies during the school year.
BKF920

Take Time for You
Tina H. Boogren

The key to thriving as a human and an educator rests in self-care. With *Take Time for You*, you'll discover a clear path to well-being. The author offers manageable strategies, reflection questions, and surveys that will guide you in developing an individualized self-care plan.
BKF813

Educator Wellness
Timothy D. Kanold and Tina H. Boogren

How do we bring our best selves to our students and colleagues each day? Designed as a reflective journal and guidebook, *Educator Wellness* will take you on a deep exploration where you will uncover profound answers that ring true for you.
BKG053

From Burnt Out to Fired Up
Morgane Michael

Overwhelmed teachers, this book is for you. The truth is that you can be remarkable without burning out. Drawing from the latest research and her own teaching experiences, author Morgane Michael delivers research-backed strategies to replenish your well-being and reignite your passion for your purpose.
BKG027

Visit SolutionTree.com or call 800.733.6786 to order.

Wait! Your professional development journey doesn't have to end with the last pages of this book.

We realize improving student learning doesn't happen overnight. And your school or district shouldn't be left to puzzle out all the details of this process alone.

No matter where you are on the journey, we're committed to helping you get to the next stage.

Take advantage of everything from **custom workshops** to **keynote presentations** and **interactive web and video conferencing**. We can even help you develop an action plan tailored to fit your specific needs.

Let's get the conversation started.

Call 888.763.9045 today.

SolutionTree.com